DUNGEONS & DRAGONS

HOW NOT TO GET EATEN BY OWLBEARS

A Survival Guide for the Forgotten Realms

CONTENTS

CHAPTER 1.
SURVIVING AND THRIVING

CHAPTER 2.
THE SWORD COAST AND HEARTLANDS

CHAPTER 3.
THE FROZENFAR

CHAPTER 4.
THE UNDERDARK

CHAPTER 5.
FARTHER AFIELD

CHAPTER 6.
REALMS BEYOND THE MORTAL

CHAPTER 7.
ASTRAL ADVENTURES

INTRODUCTION

MY NAME IS FALGRISS, AND I HAVE EXPLORED DUNGEONS, FACED CRANKY DRAGONS, AND CLEANED VOLO'S DISHES—ALL SO YOU DON'T HAVE TO.

———✦———

Your decision to pick up this book shows a degree of bravery, brilliance, and, might I say, extra coin that few can claim. You might be wondering what you're in for, and since I want to keep you reading, I will oblige.

Novice adventurers in Faerûn expect to encounter magical creatures and horrifying monsters and then fight them to the death. In fact, Faerûn boasts places full of wonder, as well as fantastical beings worth getting to know and understand deeply, THEN fighting to the death. A subtle, yet important difference.

As his popular writings illustrate the strengths and weaknesses of what he calls monsters, the famous adventurer Volo has done little to disabuse travelers of this notion. I should know; I'm his traveling companion.

A wyrmling of a dragonborn ranger, I stumbled upon Volo holding court at the Yawning Portal Inn. He turned to include me, a clanless nobody, in his storytelling without skipping a beat.

Witnessing his tale of daring captivate the inn's crowd, I was hooked. I soon offered him my bow and my service. That... was my mistake.

Since that time, I have assisted Volo as he shared his adventures from drawing room to throne room. Along the way, I have tasted the foods he tasted, listened to the same survivor tales he teased out of brave (and sometimes cowardly) adventurers, and trudged through the same muck he refused to get near. His best-selling Guides, though above and beyond the best of their kind, fail to cover the more practical details of traveling these great Realms, mostly because I'm the one who ends up organizing everything while he's dining with Lords.

To prove how very not-bitter I am, I decided to write my own Guide. I can't claim a fraction of Volo's talent for words, so I quaffed a few *enhance ability* potions and put together this humble tome. May it help you enjoy the best of what Faerûn has to offer, without getting eaten by owlbears.

I paid a human artist twenty gold and held this pose for three days, so I hope you like it.

WELCOME TO THE FORGOTTEN REALMS

SO YOU WANT TO BE AN ADVENTURER...

If you're already familiar with the Realms, turn the page and get started with the crucial task of staying alive. If, however, you're new here, there are some key things we'll need to run through first, if you want to live longer than five minutes.

Where?

Faerûn—that's where you're (probably) standing. It's a big place, a continent in fact. It's got forests, deserts, mountains, cities, and everything in between. All of it beautiful and hazardous in equal measure. Braver adventurers can travel farther afield—to other worlds or even other planes of existence entirely. But I wouldn't recommend it.

A party of adventurers sets out to seek their fortunes. One quick glance tells me that none of them have read this book...

Divine Intervention

Gods. The Realms has lots of them, and they can be fickle things, with ominous names like Myrkul, god of death, or Mask, god of thieves. The right prayer at the right time might just save your scales. Of course, they'll probably simply ignore you.

Expect the Unexpected

No matter how hard you try, not everyone you meet is going to like you. Some will dislike you for something trivial you didn't even know you did. Some will try to kill you just to take that fancy sword you've been absent-mindedly twirling. Knowing when to smile and when to run is rule number one.

The Rewards

They say fortune favors the brave, but bravery will only get you so far. That skull you tripped over in the dark? They probably thought they were brave, too. Read this book carefully, however, and you might be richly rewarded, both in terms of wealth and in tall tales to tell in the local tavern.

Fearful Fauna

The Realms' wildlife can be majestic, but steer well clear. Most of it will try to eat you, or worse. What's worse than being eaten? I'll leave that to your imagination.

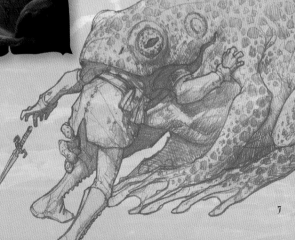

NAVIGATING THE FORGOTTEN REALMS

FROM THE SWORD COAST TO SWORDS AT YOUR THROAT: FINDING PATHS, EMBRACING CHAOS

Traversing the Forgotten Realms without research is like meeting a dragon while wearing a suit of gold coins: inadvisable. Preparing by reading this book shows impeccable taste, or a keen desire to save your own hide. Either way, with terrain and laws sometimes changing by the block, or even underfoot, any help counts.

KEY INFO

Economy: Even in a market where you can barter a song for enchanted beans, nothing beats the reassuring clink of gold coins.

Religion: The gods are as hands-on as a pickpocket in a crowded tavern, prone to a pinch too much of divine intervention for anyone's taste. Except for you, Deneir. You're great.

Population: No matter how exotic you think you are, someone's already seen three of you before breakfast. Most locals will simply nod and ask if you're going to buy anything. See Economy, above.

Magic: It's everywhere. The solution for everything and the go-to excuse for every unopened door, every floating castle, and every talking owlbear that doesn't like your attitude.

MAPS (MAKING & READING)

For those who can't follow tracks (Volo), and for those who refuse to ask directions (also Volo), you must make maps. This much-neglected duty usually falls to whoever loses arm-wrestling with the barbarian or an argument with Volo (somehow always me). Reading the map later? That's an art. Squint at your scribbles and hope. It's all part of the charm of being an intrepid, albeit occasionally lost, adventurer.

TIP: HOLD IT RIGHT SIDE UP!

Group map-making: where "X marks the spot" becomes "X marks the argument" and the real treasure is the friends you annoyed along the way.

A detailed map, but silent on lurking monsters. Adventure, yes; visual warnings, no.

Volo calls these spokes arcane ley lines. I think the cartographer wanted to charge him extra.

THAY →

The Endless Ice Sea

Reghed Glacier

ICEWIND DALE

THE SPINE OF THE WORLD

MIRABAR

LUSKAN

River Mirar

The Crags

The Lurkwood

The Glimmerwood

MITHRAL HALL

NESME

SILVERMOON

CITADEL FELBAR

CITADEL ADBAR

NETHER MOUNTAINS

SWORD MOUNTAINS

NEVERWINTER

LONGSADDLE

Neverwinter Wood

The Evermoors

EVERLUND

NETHER MOUNTAINS

TRIBOAR

YARTAR

The Lost Peaks

The Star Mounts

A n a u r o c h

The High Forest

WESTBRIDGE

LEILON

Kryptgarden Forest

RED LARCH

Dessarin River

The Far Forest

The Long Road

WATERDEEP

The High Road

Dessarin River

LOUDWATER

LLORKH

GREYPEAK MOUNTAINS

PARNAST

The Black Road

SECOMBER

South Wood

The High Moor

Serpent's Tail Stream

Serpent Hills

Mere of Dead Men

The Lonely Moor

GREY CLOAK HILLS

Sea of Swords

DAGGERFORD

The Trade Way

Serpent Hills

Mount Hotenow

Forlorn Forest

THE SHAERADIM

DRAGONSPEAR

Najara

HILL OF LOST SOULS

DALELANDS →

Mintarn

Tomb Mountain

THE TROLL HILLS

TROLLCLAWS

Winding Water

Forest of Wyrms

SOUBAR

BATTLE OF BONES

AMN & CALIMSHAN

The Fields of the Dead

Trielta Hills

TRIEL

DARKHOLD

Skull Gorge

WELL OF DRAGONS

BALDUR'S GATE

Chionthar River

SCORNUBEL

ELTUREL

N

THE SWORD COAST

Reaching Wood

Coast Way

CANDLEKEEP

BEREGOST

The Wood of Sharp Teeth

BERDUSK

SUNSET MOUNTAINS

Marsh of Tun

IRIABOR

EASTING

GREENEST

TO AMN

Framed maps? They've never faced a dungeon. Look for ones with creases and a splash of unidentified blood.

This fine Sword Coast map stands out: a rarity where each road and river aligns with reality, unlike its often bewildering brethren.

9

CHAPTER 1.
SURVIVING AND THRIVING

KNOW YOUR ROLE

✦

WHEN WORDS FAIL, SWORDS SPEAK: A CRASH COURSE IN CONTROLLED CHAOS

Warriors come in all shapes and sizes: front-line fighters, raging barbarians, or disciplined monks. Rangers and assassins bring artistry to the battlefield, one long shot and sudden silence at a time. Knowing your teammates means understanding when to charge forward and when to... meditate?

Do barbarians come from the North...

or a state of mind?

Barbarian

Masters of the mighty rage, barbarians hit battle like a storm, if the storm had muscles and a really big axe. Their version of subtlety involves choosing the slightly smaller tree to use as a club.

BEWARE THE SMELL!

Their armor takes the hits so you don't have to

DON'T TOUCH THE HOLY SYMBOL!

The bigger the shield, the more they're compensating for something.

CROSSBOWS ARE CHEATING

Fighter

Armed with every weapon, they juggle swords and enemies' fates with equal flair, asking "Why specialize when you can be an arsenal?" Slap on some armor, send them in, then sit back and watch them go.

Paladin

They heal, they shield, they lecture evil with a sword, then they serve justice with a side of armor polish. Whatever deity they follow, their moral compass always points to "smite."

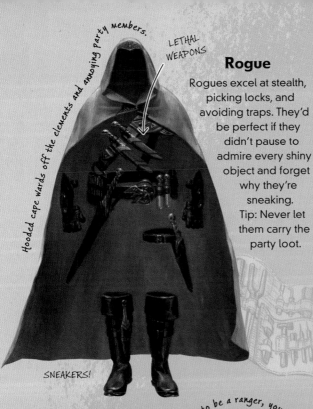

Hooded cape wards off the elements and annoying party members.

LETHAL WEAPONS

SNEAKERS!

Rogue

Rogues excel at stealth, picking locks, and avoiding traps. They'd be perfect if they didn't pause to admire every shiny object and forget why they're sneaking. Tip: Never let them carry the party loot.

Don't mind the clothes; monks are lethal even when stark naked. Enjoy!

Monk

Masters of martial arts, monks draw on their ki to hone their bodies and perfect the long, hard stare. They can catch arrows, which saves on buying them. The quiet sort, they prefer fist-to-face communication.

If you're going to be a ranger, you need to like green.

Solo, rangers are masters of their craft; in a party, it's like having a secret weapon that can also make a great campfire dinner.

Ranger

Wilderness connoisseurs, animal whisperers, unparalleled archers— rangers stroll through deadly forests like chameleons, if chameleons carried longbows and had an affinity for bear wrestling. With an owl for every occasion, who would choose any other role?

PACK A LOT OF THESE

NOW THAT'S A NICE BOW!

KNOW YOUR ROLE (CONTINUED)

SPELLCASTERS: WHEN FIREBALLS "SOLVE" PROBLEMS, BUT HEALERS HAVE TO FIX THE AFTERMATH.

Wizards read; warlocks bargain; sorcerers try not to explode. Meanwhile, the divine and nature magic of clerics and druids makes it all work. Do keep in mind that stepping on a wizard's robe or interrupting a druid's plant chat might get you turned into a toad.

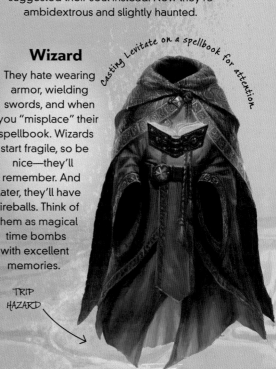

Working the whole "tortured (lack of soul)" look.

Warlock

Warlocks whisper sweet nothings to otherworldly beings and get arcane secrets in return. When they said, "I'd give my right arm for power," a demon suggested their soul instead. Now they're ambidextrous and slightly haunted.

Wizard

They hate wearing armor, wielding swords, and when you "misplace" their spellbook. Wizards start fragile, so be nice—they'll remember. And later, they'll have fireballs. Think of them as magical time bombs with excellent memories.

Casting Levitate on a spellbook for attention.

SORCERERS' MOST COMMON LAST WORDS

"Wait, no, that's not what I meant to do!"

Sorcerer

Sorcerers didn't choose the arcane life; it showed up at birth and now refuses to leave. For these adventuring hopefuls, spells come easier than explanations. They're walking, talking magical accidents waiting to happen.

TRIP HAZARD

Jaunty hat not a requirement

(But doesn't hurt!)

Cleric

They heal, they bless, they bludgeon with gusto. Sought after like the last piece of cake, clerics balance saving lives with occasionally taking them. To recruit, promise extra coin —for their temple, of course.

Armor so holy, even rust spots claim divine purpose.

Healers aren't just walking bandages; they buff, take the hits, and then begrudgingly stitch you back together after you poked the dragon. Again.

Bard

Armed with a rapier in one hand and a flute in the other, bards weave magic through song, or simply their charm. They battle with ballads, sometimes so persistently that friends and foes yield just to escape the encore.

Hooded cape with horns only wards off other deer, probably.

COULD'VE BEEN A RANGER!

Druids can cast the Shillelagh cantrip in order to say, "Behold, my magically buffed twig!"

Druid

Rangers' cousins who chose shapeshifting over sharpshooting. They share a love for the wild, but druids take "becoming one with nature" quite literally—sometimes as an oak. Cross them and they will send the whole forest after you.

15

EQUIPMENT AND GEAR

FROM CAVES TO CASTLES: MUST-HAVES FOR ALL ADVENTURERS

Some adventurers start with barely enough silver for a rusty dagger. But never fear, soon you'll be wondering who's in the market for a used, only-swung-a-few-times mace, because lo and behold, a fire giant dropped a legendary Flamesword! Dungeon loot: the real reason adventurers never settle!

SCALES FOR THOSE LACKING SCALES

Too clanky for my taste.

Not only will they hear you coming, they'll be practically deafened.

Plate armor

Ring mail

KEY INFO

Variety: Packing both melee and ranged weapons could mean the difference between a tactical retreat and just plain running for your life.

Magical equipment: Not just for wizards! A glowing sword impresses more than mere tavern crowds, and saves you from having to buy silver for those annoying werewolves.

Maintain your gear: Reinforce your backpack seams—spilled gear is a siren song for thieves. If you neglect your sword, it might just sulk and decide to fall to pieces at precisely the wrong moment.

Armor

Plate armor: for those aspiring to be fortresses with legs. Chain mail: for those seeking greater mobility (or playing rattle backup for the bard.) Wizards and sorcerers? They just wear their confidence (and maybe a mystical robe). Speaking personally, I find leather armor is the perfect silent partner for when you need to climb a tree and still look *magnificent*.

Weapons

In the armory, your choice reveals a lot about you: a sword for the bold, a wand for the wise, a dagger for the underhanded, and for the best, a longbow—no need to get close when you can make your point from a hundred feet away. Plus it saves getting blood splashed on your cloak which, trust me, is a nightmare to get out.

Shield never hurts, though!

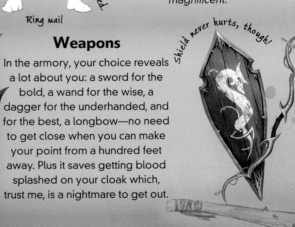

DO / DO NOT

- **DO NOT** rely on your party for essentials; you'll end up in the dark, realizing you forgot both the torches and the wizard.

- **DO** invest in quality, or your heroic tale will turn into a cautionary one about budget shopping in the Underdark.

- **DO NOT** overload. Mobility beats having a spare anvil.

Strong box

Rope

Grapple

Map

Coin purse

Cards

Ingredients

Lamp

Coins

Banner of allegiance

Scabbard

Mortar and pestle

Magic amulet

Animal familiar

Toy (great for dealing with gnomes!)

Carpentry tools

Other Useful Equipment

Beyond these usuals, bring a mirror to peek around corners, signal allies, or check your horns after battle; a compass that points to the nearest tavern (self-explanatory); and an Immovable Rod for traps or for keeping your map still while arguing with Volo.

Letter of marque

Dice

Water bottle (very important!)

Sickle (for gathering ingredients)

Fishing gear

Tinkering tools

Magical axes: Very useful when disarming—or dishanding—shadow demons.

No one likes a mace to the face!

Clubs: For when you've lost all your other weapons.

The real holy symbols of a cleric...

Bludgeoning for skeletons, slashing for thick hides, or piercing for armored foes—tailor your terror!

17

MAGIC ITEMS

WANDS, WONDERS, AND OOPS-WAS-THAT-SUPPOSED-TO-EXPLODE?

Magic items deliver the extraordinary, like a Wand of Fireballs for the overzealous, or a Cloak of Invisibility for the shy. From the Boots of Speed to the wise-cracking Sword of Sharpness, adventurers rely on these wonders for feats from battling liches to snagging the last piece of pie without being seen.

Defensive magic rings: for wizards who are sad they cannot wear leather armor.

Magic staffs: Never certain if they wield magic or are for show. Volo owns five.

A Ring of Fire Elemental Command: will get your dinner cooked, although there are easier and safer ways.

Cat's Eye Circlet: for humans who can't see past their nose in the dark it's perfect for midnight strolls in the Underdark.

Regis's Ruby Pendant: for when a halfling needs a little extra stolen charm in negotiations.

Choices, choices!

Magic Gear

Don't just settle for magic arms and armor when wizards have crafted items for the most discerning: Bags of Holding for hoarders, Capes of the Mountebank for flashy exits, and Gloves of Thievery for those "borrowing" moments. Care tip: avoid overstuffing bags, or you'll need a map to find your favorite caltrop.

Bag of Holding

FEATHER OF DIATRYMA SUMMONING

Jarlaxle's hat of disguise: The height of spy fashion, it also allows Jarlaxle to summon a protective giant bird (or, alternatively, a beard).

Magic Weapons

Magical weapons can do far more than successfully strike wererats. Some swords blaze with fire for those who like their battles well-done. Some arrows crackle with lightning, so watch where you aim. And certain daggers drip with venom, for when you need to make a long and lingering point.

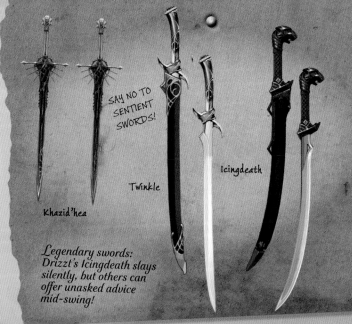

SAY NO TO SENTIENT SWORDS!

Khazid'hea

Twinkle

Icingdeath

Legendary swords: Drizzt's Icingdeath slays silently, but others can offer unasked advice mid-swing!

The Mirror of Life Trapping: captures anything, from dragons to nagging neighbors. Handy, unless you end up trapped in it yourself.

Powerful and Dangerous!

Some magic items are not to be trifled with. The Deck of Many Things tops the list—using it is like playing cards with fate itself. Then there's the Sphere of Annihilation, perfect for when you really, really don't like a wall. The Wand of Orcus? It lies to its wielder, intends to slay all, and worse, has zero sense of humor.

Here's looking at you...

The Eye of Vecna: will let you cast some crazy powerful spells, but at a heavy cost (you'll need an empty socket to put it in...)

Deck of Many Things: you gamble with a fate worse than death every time you draw a card.

Crenshinibon: a sun-powered, power-hungry crystal shard, luring unwary mages with grand false promises. (What did I say about sentient items? No! Bad!)

A GUIDE

ON THE ROAD

HIGHWAYS AND BYWAYS: MEANDERING MERRILY (AND SOMETIMES HAIRILY) ACROSS THE MAP

Maybe your wizard's *teleport* spell fizzled, or your griffon caught a cold. So what if a journey by road adds hours, if not days to your journey? It beats slogging through marshland with shoes full of swamp soup. Getting there may not be half the adventure, but the whole of it.

Auroch

Metallic dragon

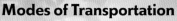

Axe beak

NOTHING LIKE RIDING A LIVING, BREATHING SIEGE ENGINE

Modes of Transportation

Choose your ride carefully: metallic dragons for when you're feeling ostentatious; axe beaks for zippy escapes. Caravans attract those who love a good natter, while stagecoaches are the worst unless you enjoy bumpy "Are we flying?" experiences. War wagons are perfect for those with enemies, or who are expecting trouble.

I WAS STUCK IN A CARAVAN WITH VOLO ONCE. NEVER AGAIN!

Stagecoach

War wagon

Caravan

Nothing like a good ol' bridge ambush, where the biggest concern isn't the goblins above, but the bugbear beneath.

Top Tip: send the ranger in your party to check the bridge first!

Night watch: where an elf's "I don't need sleep" meets "I didn't volunteer for this."

Camping

Pick the safest-looking spot and then... don't camp there. That's where Gertie the owlbear camps. Once you find an actual safe spot, light a campfire to keep the creatures away. But be warned—fires are also top-notch at summoning uninvited storytelling bards. Consider casting *wards* a distance from the tents. You never know who might be approaching, and not just the aforementioned bard.

Finding or Making Shelter

Consider your shelter options. An inn offers a bed, but also overpriced ale. Making your own bed? Free, if you don't mind the occasional bear. Find a friendly treant, convince it you're not a woodchuck, and boom—instant shelter. Or try a cave—but avoid the ones with snoring.

BEWARE!

On the main roads of Faerûn, watch for bandits with ambitions larger than yours. A goblin raiding party could turn your epic quest into an unheroic trip back to town, broke. And if you haven't dodged a rain of fire by a fly-by dragon, have you even truly lived? Sometimes the road less traveled means a lot less singeing.

Treant

MAGICAL MISHAPS

DANGEROUS FOR MAGIC-USERS, MUCH WORSE FOR ANYONE AROUND THEM

Ever tried casting *detect thoughts* and ended up hearing only tavern songs for days? Did your effort at alchemy misfire and transmute your gold into cheese? (Kind of a brilliant outcome, actually.) Rest assured, in the grand scheme of magic, you're in good, albeit occasionally cheese-handed, company.

What happens when you accidentally swap potions...

KEY INFO

Spell components: Like baking, but with more fireballs. Always double-check your ingredients —mistaking salt for sulfur can lead to explosively bad dinners. Wizards advise carrying a surplus of eye of newt. No reason, they just like being mysterious.

Know your zones: Wild magic zones? Nature's pranksters, where spells turn into a game of magical roulette. No magic zones? Even better. There you can wave your wand all you want, but you'll just be an eccentric person with a fancy stick.

Potions

Identifying potions can be risky guesswork. Find a potion in a goblin's pocket? Could be *healing*, or turn you into a toad just in time for your long weekend. Wizards warn against guess-sipping; that's why they invented identification spells. Potion shopping? Beware of discounts—that *elixir of strength* might just be ogre sweat.

For best results, follow these potion brewing tips: Stir clockwise for healing, counterclockwise for invisibility, and never lick the spoon afterward.

BEWARE!

Magic can turn you from ally to enemy in a heartbeat. Miscalculate a spell's area of effect and you'll have to embark on an apology tour for singeing the rogue's eyebrows. Fall for a charm spell and you might end up buying swampland in the Underdark with your party's gold. And flashy spells? Great for attracting every guard in a fifty-foot radius. It's like shouting "Sneaky party right here!" Cast responsibly.

Hazardous Spells

Spells like *lightning bolt* present obvious hazards, especially when standing in water, but don't count out those "non-offensive" spells. One wrong *teleport* and you've skipped the teeth straight into a dragon's stomach. *Wish* for your own castle and you may end up enjoying a sandcastle. In the desert. Without water. Be careful what you wish for.

Sure, you summoned him. But does he look happy to see you?

Dangerous Rituals

Step one, draw complex symbols; step two, chant, wave hands, avoid tripping on robes; step three, accidentally invite extra-planar beings over for a heart-to-heart. To stop a ritual, disrupt the eerie chanting with a tasteful joke. And if your ritual risks ending the world, make sure it's for something greater than a deep clean of your hideout.

Rare mystic dust

FLOUR WORKS TOO!

Circle crafting for rituals: symmetry is key. An uneven circle might mean the difference between summoning a dragon and summoning a dragoon.

Levitating is super fun until someone casts dispel magic.

NECROMANCY

Despite its name, some necromancy spells are quite neighborly, like *spare the dying*. But *animate dead*? That's a hard no from me. Cross that line, and I'll judge you from both sides of the grave. Get consent first. You are free to cast *speak with dead* on me, as long as you're not the reason I'm available for a hello!

SOCIAL SURVIVAL
OR HOW TO WIN FRIENDS BY LYING TO PEOPLE

There are a lot of scary things in this book. But none of them are as scary as social interaction. Sure, a mind flayer will eat your brain, but mess up at a gala and people will *laugh* at you. I've learned a lot from watching Volo, so here's how to avoid the worst death of all—a social one.

Not a dagger in sight.

Can still stab you in the back.

The rich call it a masquerade...

...THE POOR CALL IT ROBBERY

If you have avoided the great misfortune of noble birth, study this ostentatious pose so you can better blend in.

Navigating High Society

It's not only about bards charming secrets out of snooty patriars. A wizard's botched spells can make for dazzling, if unintended, party tricks. Turn your flubs into social triumphs— just mind the occasional fireball faux pas!

If you encounter Duchess Saidra in Dementlieu, compliment her mask, then slowly back away (ideally from the Domains of Dread altogether).

How it looks when the Gralhunds of Waterdeep are plotting to sell you out for gold.

At the Grand Masquerade, a fancy costume could mean the difference between having a wonderful evening and getting swept up in a dustpan.

Know your neighborhood. Old Money means ancestors get name-dropped more than spells. New Money trends to the flashy, with diamonds for all—except you specifically.

Hint: One carriage can carry 50,000 gold pieces.

Those who run away live to run away another day. This is Volo's preferred method, second only to boring them to death.

Failed to impress that lug three times larger than you? Pivot! Compliment their hairstyle, whip out your cute pseudodragon, or start an impromptu history quiz. Confusion is your best friend in these moments.

Dealing with Confrontation

If charm—or your bard—flops, challenge adversaries to a thumb war or time an *illusion* spell to turn any argument into a puppet show! You will still fail, but at least someone will be entertained (namely me, if you follow this advice).

An orc's eyesight is good, but they can't charge what they don't see.

Even the smoothest talkers may find that words weigh less than a good longsword and the will to use it.

Stealth and Evasion

Sometimes the best conversation is none at all. Blending into tapestries, mimicking statues, mastering the art of being unnoticeably noticeable all keep you two steps ahead. And when push comes to shove, a quick "Look behind you!" still works wonders, especially if your rogue ally is hiding in the shadows.

Hidden heists and quiet takedowns clean up messy business, and allow society to pretend like nothing happened.

The drow of Bregan Daerthe are like invisible, deadly butlers: always there, never seen, and making problems disappear, all while avoiding the dreaded dance floor.

SHOPPING

HOW TO SHOP LIKE AN ARCHMAGE AND SPEND LIKE A PEASANT

Buying a map can turn into a treasure hunt, while haggling over a potion might reveal a hidden conspiracy. Magic in the marketplace proves more likely than a good deal on rations. Whatever your poison, your shopping list says more about you than your diary ever could.

KEY INFO

Currency matters: Your wallet jingles with gold, silver, and copper, but a well-spun tale might just seal the deal.

Location matters: Seeking celestial armor? Your neighborhood blacksmith may fall short, but the Astral Plane beckons!

Market matters: You won't find spell scrolls at the blacksmith, nor masterwork weapons at the alchemist's. If you're after an infernal war machine, first, what's wrong with you? and second, only the Wandering Emporium can supply.

BUYING MAGIC ITEMS

1

Verify an item is magic: A detect magic spell works better than asking a nearby goblin for their opinion.

2

Determine an item's effect: Maybe test the alchemist's fire outside the shop, first.

3

Pick a price: Be ready to part with your gold —dragons aren't the only ones who hoard.

You won't find your next armor here, but you might find a sweet tea or poison.

The real treasure is in not getting duped.

Deep gnomes attempting to negotiate a two down to a one, while drow heckle... probably.

Inter-Species Etiquette

In the market, forewarned is forearmed, so know who you're buying from or selling to. Elves tend to browse with eternal patience, while a dwarf admires craftsmanship, not your haggling skills. Offer a gnome a gadget, and you've made a friend. And never, ever cut in line.

"Good" Deals

Be careful of merchants insisting their dragon's-hoard-priced torches are the best deal in the Underdark, because it's, well, dark. Or do wares seem a little too cheap? They might be a literal steal! And watch out for that bargain spellbook with surprise side effects—or enjoy your new duck feet, no extra charge!

BEWARE!

Fraudulent sellers abound, peddling wands that couldn't cast a shadow or cursed items with more strings attached than a puppet theater. Shop in the wrong alley and discover your coin pouch practicing the art of disappearance. Exclusive stores guard their goods like a salamander protecting its eggs—fiercely and with fire. Shop smart, or your remains may be the next sale!

A veritable cabinet of poisonous curiosities.

Buying potions saves on cleaning up after trying to make them yourself.

Need ingredients like dragon scales? Buying them spares you the awkwardness of trying to seduce your dragonborn traveling companion.

Smiles are just lies with teeth.

ABOUT TO
CON YOU!

The Art of the Haggle

Where "win-win" means "I win twice." First, knowing your potion's true worth beats guessing, so come prepared. Start fair, but avoid pushing too hard or the shopkeeper might just keep more than the shop. Charm them right, though, and prices drop faster than a clumsy rogue in a pit trap.

ALLIES AND COMPANIONS

MAKING FRIENDS (AND LIKELY A FEW ENEMIES) IN THE REALMS

Practice the subtle art of choosing allies. Pick the gnome who's always there, even if only for the snacks. Avoid anyone who thinks they're the next Volo (we are the worst, I'm afraid). Embrace the quiet one; their best ideas usually emerge after the louder plans have, quite literally, exploded in everyone's face.

All you need for a solid adventure: the scholar, the strategist, the braveheart...

Planning the attack: a timeless saga. Choose companions you'd enjoy eternity with!

...and the rogue enamored with his shiny dagger.

Bard

Barbarian

The Skill Set Buffet

For the most effective of parties, ensure a diversity of talents: a magic adept to decode mystical gibberish, a sleight of hand expert for when pockets need lightening, and a nature guru who can tell if a plant is a healer's dream or just salad dressing for an owlbear. Variety is, as they say, the spice of life (and the best way to avoid a horrible death).

Wizard

Cleric

Too bad you can't just keep the owl.

Allies who have familiars mean you get two for one party members—whether you like it or not!

MAKING FRIENDS STEP-BY-STEP

1

The old standby: Sit broodingly by the fire in the inn just right so you can lure fellow adventurers into your party, but remember genuine connections come from shared goals, values, and taste in ale.

2

Trust, but eavesdrop: When a charismatic traveler suggests a wild quest, run a quick background check with the locals. Do not automatically listen to the explorer who invites you to travel with him to see the world. I don't care if he is Volo.

3

If all else fails, bribes: Gold is too basic. Why not offer a freshly baked pie to get the best room at the inn?

BEWARE!

Not all allies are friends. Choose your informants as you would magical artifacts: with a mix of hope and suspicion. Trust them as far as a gnome can throw a dragon, and always be ready for the inevitable twist. In this world of intrigue, even the walls have ears, and sometimes they snitch!

Odd Couples

A stealthy rogue pairs with a clanking, armor-clad knight—the ultimate game of "hide and clang." A wizard ponders ancient tomes while a gung-ho barbarian "punctuates" points with a warhammer. Unlikely allies? Sure. Unforgettable, if slightly awkward, adventures? Absolutely!

What could an orc and a kobold be bonding over? I'm not sure, but I doubt you'd find it quite as amusing as they do.

29

IMPORTANT FACTIONS

FAERÛN'S FINEST (AND FAR FROM FINEST): A GUIDE TO ITS MOST INFLUENTIAL GROUPS

Enjoy the feast of factions, where the Harpers whisper secrets under the table as the Zhentarim grab for the biggest piece of pie. The Order of the Gauntlet is arguing ethics with the sofa, while the Emerald Enclave is outside, befriending a tree. Pass the diplomacy, please!

Lords' Alliance

Noble rulers from Waterdeep to Neverwinter have formed an elite club of strategy and intrigue. They recruit only the most loyal bards, paladins, and mages, who discreetly battle evil while trying not to trip over their own ornate cloaks.

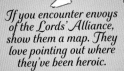

If you encounter envoys of the Lords' Alliance, show them a map. They love pointing out where they've been heroic.

Lords' Alliance signet ring

Wave it around—doors (and possibly treasure chests) not-so-magically open!

Too stodgy for my tastes.

Harpers

Champions of the downtrodden, Harper agents work alone and communicate by secret signs and sounds. So secret, one might be standing right behind you, plotting against tyrants while they judge your choice in tavern snacks.

Sleight of dagger! It hides a Harper whistle.

WHEN YOU'RE SHORT ONE HARP...

Order of the Gauntlet

Where evil gets a prompt, no-nonsense smiting. Members are part paladin, part monk, all action, zero hesitation, and follow a strict "no evil tolerated" policy. They make surprisingly delightful dinner guests. Must be all that righteousness.

Half toolbelt, half garden, this Emerald Enclave bracer is just the thing for when you need to prune mid-battle.

A moving stronghold of the Order, armed with faith and an appetite for justice.

FIRES

POISON, MEDICINE

SIGNAL MIRROR

POISON HERBS

Emerald Enclave

Led by eco-enthusiast druids, dedicated to keeping nature untamed yet safe. Members can chat with blink dogs here and there, and turn a dire bear's growls into mere grumbles. They're not tree-huggers; they're tree negotiators!

Zhentarim weapons wear their own sneers.

Zhentarim

A criminal band of rogues and spellcasters, they see rules as mere stepping stones to greatness. They navigate Faerûn with a wink, a nudge, and a well-placed coin, always ready to offer a "helping hand"... to themselves.

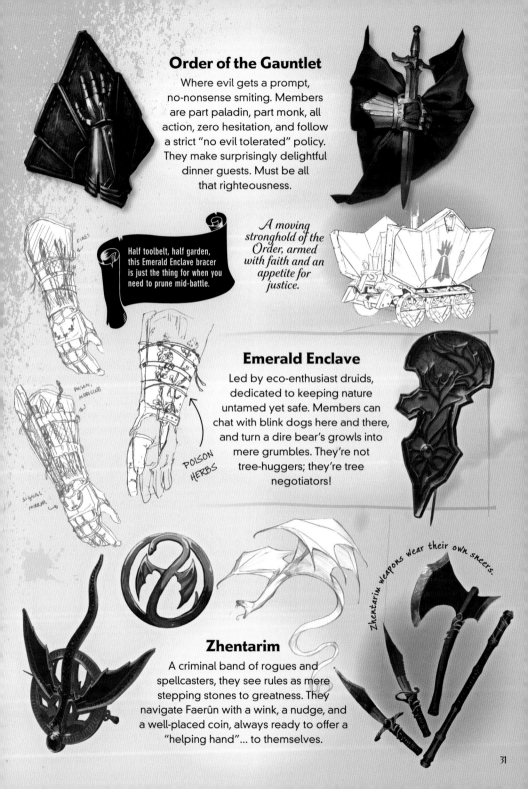

CRIME AND PUNISHMENT

THIEVERY: A CAREER PATH WITH TWISTS AND TURNS THAT USUALLY LEAD TO A DUNGEON

Sure, you could grab what you fancy from those too rich to keep track of their treasure, but at least they really deserve it. Oh, what was I saying? Ah, yes. Crime pays, sometimes, but be warned—it often pays in ways you don't want, like the opportunity to decorate your new cell with those exquisite stolen tapestries.

Rope-dropping into the salon: for when you need that priceless artifact, but your dinner invitation got lost.

If you're arrested, enjoy the free parade in your honor, complete with judgmental townfolk and the clanking of the guard as accompaniment.

A Life of Crime

On the plus side, you'll never need to worry about the coin in your pocket; you can always steal more. However, don't expect a life of luxury and leisure to ensue. You'll find the worst part to be the endless errands for unpleasant crime bosses, or dodging those irked by your financial independence!

Actually, this is the worst part.

Ah, murder—where the clues are often plenty, but the answers few.

FEIGN CLUMSINESS, GRAB GOLD

Master the art of pickpocketing and impress friends with unplanned wealth redistribution. Just don't get caught!

The vacant stare of a typical watchman.

The badge of the Waterdeep City Watch: a signal to put any shady doings on hold until they've passed by.

In Waterdeep, the City Guard guards the gate and walls (and their own asses).

Watching the Watchmen

Most city watches mix keen-eyed humans, burly dwarves, and elves who patrol the streets with a swagger only a too-tight helmet can give. Fluent in "Suspicious Glance," they navigate alleys better than many thieves, possibly because a few of them are on the take, so put your bribing pants on. Incredibly, they all apparently dislike donuts.

Prisons and Dungeons

Lawbreaking offers unique perks, like complimentary accommodation in the local dungeon, complete with iron-bar views. You can even make lifelong friends. Which may not be that long if you fail to bribe the guards. And if you've been *really* bad, expect to find yourself in Revel's End (shown above), where you'll be treated to the spectacle of watching your chamber pot freeze solid in front of you.

The Waterdeep City Watch: less shiny than the Guard, they eschew fancy weapons, preferring the art of persuasive truncheons.

BIG FOLK (AKA GIANTS)

ANCIENT RULERS WITH BIG HEARTS, BUT NOT NECESSARILY BIG SENTIMENTS

The giants' god, Annam, gave them the celestial cold shoulder for losing their grip on the world. Now they're on a mission to impress their sulky deity, but with all the grace of elephants. They follow the ordning, their version of gentility, where betrayal isn't evil, just a giant, giant faux pas.

Storm Giants

Standing atop the ordning, the mighty storm giants are the greatest of giantkind. From their underwater or cloud-based castles, they forecast doom and gloom while doing naught about it.

Cloud Giants

Noble with a mischievous streak, these sky aristocrats bet on mortal fates and consider getting caught cheating part of the fun. They climb the ordning ladder by flaunting their wealth—because coin, not character, is king!

About to throw down a sweet bolt.

A floating disk spell proves impervious to a cloud giant's wind, unlike axes and adventurers.

Fire Giants

These militaristic giants live in volcanoes, forge metalwork in the cradle, train in lava playgrounds, and plot conquests with hammer in one hand and strategy in the other.

Not just warmongers, but skilled crafter warmongers.

Angry fire giant = run!

Living a dream life...

...by making sure you're not in it.

Stone Giants

Underground, these hermits sculpt epic dramas in stone and toss boulders to show off their upper arm strength. Above ground, they treat life like a dream, heedless that it really hurt when they dropped that boulder on your head.

Hill Giants

For these brutes, size matters. Brains... not so much. Their idea of a fine meal is anything that doesn't run away fast enough, and the biggest belly leads the charge. Outsmart them subtly, or face a giant-sized tantrum!

ABOUT TO DINE ON AN ADVENTURER

Frost Giants

These bullies of the tundra love a good tavern-smashing spree. They suffer a serious case of dragonborn envy, prizing dragonscale amor and dragon's tooth mauls more than any single raided village. Wrestling for leadership? It's their version of social climbing.

For a frost giant, every hard-won scar is a step up the ordning.

DRAGONS

HOW TO IDENTIFY THE DRAGON THAT'S ABOUT TO EAT YOU

PROBABLY TOO LATE...

Eons ago, the goddess Tiamat thought, "Why not dragon?," and Faerûn's been dealing with the scaly consequences ever since. The chromatic dragons are the ones you need to watch out for. These winged wonders love treasure hoards, destruction, and the occasional terrified villager. If you hear a roar, it's not your stomach.

NOT a self-portrait. I couldn't torch a village if I tried. Not saying I did.

Breath weapon = Fire

Hoarding gold and roasting paladins in their volcano lair comes naturally to my kin, alas. They sport scales like lava, hearts like stone, and their hospitality... well, that part needs work.

RED DRAGONS

"Nice horn, but we're no reds!"— every blue dragon, probably.

Breath weapon = Lightning

Blue dragons have sky-high egos, but rather cozy ground-level lairs. Their charge is simply stunning and and they dazzle with sapphire scales, but their tempers? A true sandstorm.

BLUE DRAGONS

Breath weapon = Gas

Masters of the woods, green dragons mix charm and cunning into a poison they live and breathe. They'll talk your ear off as they plot your surprise farewell party.

GREEN DRAGONS

Breath weapon = Acid

With acidic attitude best matched with a swampy lair aesthetic, black dragons love a good soak—in the tears of their foes. They'll melt your heart, literally.

BLACK DRAGONS

Metallic dragons

A far cry from their dodgy chromatic kin, metallic dragons collect artifacts and judgments with equal fervor, their hoards a hodgepodge of heirlooms and hasty conclusions. Still, they'd donate it all to save a kidnapped innocent. Gold dragons are like heroic knights minus the clanking armor, while silvers hold the record for longest monologue. Bronze, brass, and copper dragons, meanwhile, love justice, good conversation, and well crafted pranks, respectively.

Prowling frosty peaks, white dragons love sparkly diamonds and snowball fights, because they always win. For them, eternal winter isn't just a weather forecast, it's a lifestyle.

Breath weapon = Cold

WHITE DRAGONS

LEGENDARY NASTIES

FEARSOME FOES AND WHERE TO FLEE THEM

These horrors don't do "forever gone"; they prefer "see you next century." Running away screaming may seem better than becoming their next chew toy, but their unfettered reigns of terror are far, far worse. Whether you opt for fight or flight, remember that you and yours living long, happy lives is the real victory, especially when these villains' return ticket is always booked.

Vecna

Undead Overachiever. His goal is godhood and universal domination, and he already managed the first part. Armed with legendary resistance as well as Afterthought (his trusty dagger), Vecna's the lich who makes death seem like a brief pause, and evil like his daily journal entry.

Vecna leaves his Book of Vile Darkness, his eye, and his hand (pictured) just lying around. Not only evil, unsanitary.

Acererak

Tomb Architect Extraordinaire. Has fewer fanatical followers than Vecna, but his work (and his victims) screams infamy. Think legendary dungeons like the Tomb of Horrors and Tomb of Annihilation. Body destroyed? No rush, he'll reform and plot revenge at a leisurely pace. Cares less about fame, more about crafting deadly dungeons and draining adventurers' souls for a lich's version of fun.

Know Your Lich: Spot Acererak by his Staff of the Forgotten One, which bears the skull of one of his old enemies. Take care or you might become the next in line for skulldom.

Demogorgon

Straight from the Abyss, this demon lord turns chaos into a never-ending job and makes other villains look like amateurs. His two heads mean double the mayhem, each with a gaze that's either "daze" or "craze." He plots to turn the multiverse into his personal whirlpool of confusion, if only he can stop arguing with himself.

Tiamat

FIVE HEADS FIVE!

Keen to usher in an Age of Dragons, evil dragon goddess Tiamat is better off trapped in Avernus in The Nine Hells, or literally anywhere but Faerûn. Those trying to unleash her need a serious hobby. Awkward truth: without this Mother of Dragons, there'd be no me, but I'd work tirelessly against her—so joke's on her, I guess?

Terrifying, but cheer up! At least it isn't your grandma trying to kill you.

Not sure if this is a smirk or not?

The Tarrasque

A cataclysm on two legs, this titan occasionally wakes up from a long rest to remind everyone why it's the stuff of nightmares and divine judgment. It shrugs off magic like rain, and mirrors it back with a smirk. This harbinger of doom turns towns into appetizers and uses adventurers as floss.

MONSTER SPOTTER'S GUIDE

Cities and Dungeons

Encounter a Black Pudding and take a lesson in why not to wear your favorite armor. Watch your step—this demon lord sludge loves ceiling ambushes almost as much as melting your gear!

BLACK PUDDING

These beasts follow death's perfume, and if they find none, will happily whip up their own batch. Excellent hosts, they offer uninvited guests a touch of paralysis and the promise of being tomorrow's leftovers.

CARRION CRAWLER

Where Black Puddings are metal munchers, Gelatinous Cubes are the all-inclusive dungeon cleaners, engulfing debris, adventurers, and dreams whole. They leave nothing behind but sparkles and a slow, agonizing death.

PERFECT FOR AN OGRE'S DRINK, THOUGH

GELATINOUS CUBE

These aberrations enjoy a good wallow in their own (and anyone else's) filth. Champions of laziness, Otyughs lure their dinner with a telepathic hello. Their culinary motto? Everything tastes better with a dash of adventurer.

OTYUGH

Woods

ANKHEG

Nature's way of bringing excitement back to the outdoors, these monsters pop up with acid spit and a death grip, turning farmers' and adventurers' thoughts from the mundane to "Why is the ground eating me?!"

This monster burrows, waiting to feel the beat of feet on the surface. Right on cue, it leaps onto stage! And by stage, I mean you. Tread carefully, unless you want to wear one as a hat.

TOO BIG ON YOU

BULETTE

CHAPTER 2. THE SWORD COAST & HEARTLANDS

BLINK DOG

These pups can sniff out what you had for dinner last week, and they're mad you didn't share. Masters of the surprise snuggle, they teleport to outwit foes and play a mean game of fetch with themselves.

OWLBEAR

These cranky monsters are what happened when a wild wizard couldn't decide between a bear hug and an owl's wisdom, so went with both and threw in extra claws and a beak for good measure.

These sentient salads love lightning and consuming your squishy bits. That sword you were trying to defend yourself with will be left for their next applicant for victim. Watch your step, or you're shambling compost!

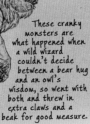

SHAMBLING MOUND

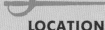
NEVERWINTER

FLOATING ON OPTIMISM, CLOUDS, AND SOMETIMES LAVA

Enjoy the audacious spirit of Neverwinter's residents, who looked at a volcano and thought, "What a fantastic place for a city!" Fear not, though, for Lord Protector Neverember has great taste in mercenaries, employing dragonborn to protect the cosmopolitan masses from the next "oopsie."

Marvel at the city's three iconic carved bridges—the Dolphin, the Winged Wyvern, and the Sleeping Dragon—arcing over the Neverwinter River. Functional, artistic, and a tad better than the rope bridges you make. In the skies, the Moonstone Mask, a floating tavern, beckons. Gamble with a tiefling, mingle with pirates, but maybe don't look down too often. It's a long way down to the city streets!

Castle Never in happier days. Now the ultimate fixer-upper due to volcano-inflicted subsidence, it stands as a proud, albeit hazardous, symbol of resilience, or of Neverember's foolishness if he thinks he can live there.

The "Jewel of the North" shows off in every way, even in the Hall of Justice, where awe can quickly turn into an unplanned incarceration.

Behold the Chasm, which prior to the Cataclysm consisted of the Beggar's Nest and Arcanist districts of the city. Mutated monsters spilled from its depths to plague the rest of Neverwinter, until it was sealed off.

THE CATACLYSM

Feeling like Neverwinter didn't take it seriously as a volcano, Mount Hotenow decided to redecorate the city in the "Gaping Hole" style with a bit of "Lake of Fire." The resulting monster–filled Chasm would have continued to prove a pedestrian hazard had not Lord Protector Neverember enlisted a few wizards to seal it up. Fast forward forty years or so and trade with Waterdeep has picked up again, proving greedy optimism reigns eternal in Neverwinter.

Neverwinter from the south

"The City of Skilled Hands" is perhaps so skilled due to rebuilding the city again and again. It includes artisans crafting clocks for those who appreciate unnerving accuracy.

Whether a doorway to the Nine Hells or the perfect red dragon hideaway, Mount Hotenow likes to keep everyone on their toasty toes.

NEVERWINTER WOOD

FROM TWIG BLIGHTS TO TWILIGHT TERRORS, IT'S THE WORLD'S LEAST RELAXING WOODLAND RETREAT

The gnarled trees of Neverwinter Wood conceal mystery and peril in equal measure. Here elves once lived and loved, then left... a few times. Avoid wielding your axe with abandon—the forest will exact its revenge in the form of whitethistle shrubbery, which imparts a humbling lesson in both botany and gastric rebellion.

Riverside saunas, anyone? Enjoy the naturally warmed Neverwinter River that makes the forest cozy all year round. Ideal for those who like their nature with a touch of underdirt heating.

Dryad striding between trees to duck boring conversations.

If she's talking to you, she probably thinks you're a plant.

Woodland Creatures

A mystical crossroads, Neverwinter Wood experiences a lot of turnover. After the elves, fey migrated in droves due to the Spellplague. Many in turn fled when marauding orcs came a-marauding. Expect to encounter fey, goblinoids, magic, and whatever spills out of the Neverwinter crypts.

BEWARE!

Adventurers seeking easy riches often target the forest's ruins, but soon discover they are taking the hard lack-of-road with secret entrances, crafty traps, and forgotten lore that might outwit the smartest wizard. If one can avoid the roaming red dragon, a cruise down Neverwinter River could lead to the reclaimed dwarven city of Gauntlgrym (above), although neither dwarves nor dragon will simply hand over their hard-wrought treasure, alas. Tip: Take the Triboar Trail instead—it's relatively dragon-free.

Follow the river in either direction and you'll end up either engulfed in molten lava or on your way over Neverwinter Falls.

HOW NOT TO GET EATEN BY OWLBEARS

1

Practice good stealth hygiene: Keeping in mind their keen senses, blend into the forest's sights and smells. Mask the fact you ate the last biscuit.

2

No midnight strolls: Owlbears hunt at night, so avoid errands after dark—think of it as nature's curfew.

3

Distraction: If you do encounter one or two, throw something (not yourself) to create a diversion. Owlbears can't resist a good chase, and it's good if it's not you.

4

Make friends?: Regularly offer it gourmet snacks (owlbear-friendly, of course). With time, you may find yourself with a powerful companion. It will still eat you, but much later.

Gertie here had a companion once.

Magical Mysteries

The fey left behind more than just footprints—including an active crossing leading straight into, and out of, the mystical realm known as the Feywild. Sharandar, the old elven keep, is shedding magic all over the forest like a dire wolf sheds fur. It's really quite messy.

45

In Baldur's Gate, merchants find respite from the Sea of Swords, trading plundering pirates for pilfering patriars.

Gray Harbor, the site of city founder Balduran's return from the Trackless Sea, annually hosts a grand fête.

BALDUR'S GATE

CITY OF COIN, AND INCREASINGLY LIGHT COIN PURSES. COME RICH, LEAVE BROKE!

Fancy a trade, a tale, or a tussle? This city's got it all, plus a chance to dodge a back-alley dagger or two!

Baldur's crest illustrates how every wave and gate slaps you with a tariff.

Baldur's Gate, strategically perched on the Chionthar River, is the go-to spot for merchants who love water views and trade tax. The largest city on the Sword Coast, it sidesteps the messy politics and conflicts of its neighbors with its neutral, no-nonsense, very tall walls. Inside, the Council of Four discusses, deliberates, and sometimes dilly-dallies. Yet below the shiny surface of the city lurk the Guild, its shadow puppeteers. With so much influence, you'd think they were the ones wearing the ducal crowns—except they prefer their crowns a bit more... invisible. In the Outer City, the rule is "build it and hope no one complains." An example being Little Calimshan, a slice of the south on the Sword Coast. The air is as filled with

WHERE TO STAY

The Blushing Mermaid

At The Blushing Mermaid you'll find beds as bouncy as a gelatinous cube, food with a dash of shady dealings, and a shortcut to the Undercellar. Hag is not on the menu, but you may get one anyway.

Helm and Cloak

The Helm and Cloak marks the spot for helms, cloaks, and a plush retreat where you can rub elbows with other merry fools.

Elfsong Tavern

With its resident ghost of a singing elf maiden, Elfsong Tavern remains the serene spot for those who like their nights as long as an elven ballad.

Wyrm´s Rock Prison

Temporarily embarrassed? You could do worse than here. Perfect if your idea of fun is gloomy walls and a menu that makes trail rations seem gourmet. A true "rock–bottom" experience!

the smell of tanneries as it is with the dreams of the downtrodden, who have all set up shop where the city's nose can't reach. But let's not forget the dark shadows that loom over the city's past, a past replete with sinister events including a monstrous transformation, a riot, and heroes stepping in to save the day... three separate times. And below its bustling streets, Ansur, the legendary undead dragon, supposedly slumbers. To locals, Ansur is the city's own bogeyman— or bogeydragon—but in Baldur's Gate, legends have a habit of waking up.

DO / DO NOT

• DO NOT slip up and call residents "Baldurans"—it's Baldurians, thank you very much.

• DO NOT mention the Lord of Murder, Bhaal. It's a sore subject, and locals prefer remembering their history with a lower body count.

• DO visit Little Calimshan for a taste and feel of the south without the months of travel (a tip for the lazy).

BALDUR'S GATE: UPPER CITY

WHERE NOBLES COMPETE IN THE ANCIENT ART OF OUT-SNUBBING EACH OTHER

Rub shoulders with Baldur's Gate elite, from the influential members of the Council of Four, like Duke Thalamra Vanthampur, to that one old guy in the Watch who just knows everyone and everything for some reason. Miss a step in high society and you'll lose your title, or worse, your fortune.

Blending in? Noble garb or Watch uniforms work, but it's the confident extra-long strides that seal the deal.

KEY INFO

Elite galas: Thinking of gatecrashing? In a crowd where everbody's a somebody, you'll be the obvious nobody. You could always save a duke's life and get an invite instead?

Elite transit: How you get there is half the social battle. Who needs carriages when you've got gilded palanquins and gem-studded walking sticks?

Elite manners: Master the art of saying nothing while speaking. Want to ruffle feathers? "How quaint!" is the equivalent of a rogue's sneak attack.

Temples District

If you want to do anything official, you'll have to visit the Temples District. At the High House of Wonders, Gond's priests tinker away, foolishly giving all the credit to their god. Meanwhile, High Hall, the Ducal Palace, doubles as a government office and a history museum, probably because even the ghosts still need to file paperwork.

Visit the Wide: mostly market, part-time festival ground. Buy an apple today for the wedding tomorrow.

THE WIDE'S MOST FAMOUS RESIDENT: A STATUE OF THE HERO MINSC

Patriars

Nobles for whom climbing the social ladder means being born on the top rung. They've got luxury, they've got decadence, and they've got looking down on the poors to an art. Some try to better the city, but most are too busy keeping up appearances.

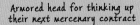

Armored head for thinking up their next mercenary contract

Fiery fist for Lower City justice

Flaming Fist

The Flaming Fist-for-hire protects the Lower City, but its prize officer, Duke Ulder Ravengard, calls the Upper City home. Joining's a breeze, especially for adventurers craving a dash of order with their chaos. Rise through the ranks swiftly and you might just trade guard duty for a dukedom.

DUKE THALAMRA VANTHAMPUR

Heroes of Baldur's Gate

Minsc and Boo, famed for hamster-powered heroics, and Jaheira, nature's fierce protector, set legendary standards. The most recent heroes? Still out celebrating (promise!) their recent victory over some big-brained monster. Volo's already telling their tale, minus his own "crowd-pleasing" near-execution.

And those "appearances" lean frumpy, evidently.

Baldur's Gate (the gate)

The city's eponymous gateway is also its most notorious tollbooth. It's the only gate between the Upper and Lower Cities that permits commoners and merchants to pass, so you can be sure the patriars use a different, riffraff-free gate. If you're not presenting a patriar's crest or carrying their shopping list, prepare to empty your pockets.

BALDUR'S GATE: LOWER CITY

WHETHER HUNTING FOR TREASURE OR TROUBLE, YOU'LL FIND IT HERE

In poor neighborhoods like Brampton, smugglers chuckle at their Upper City clientele, and probably their Bloomridge neighbors—dandies flaunting fancy swords and rooftop gardens. By day, a thousand shops clamor; by night, fog rolls in from the harbor and lantern bearers tread cautiously. It's a place where everyone has a story, but not all are eager to share.

Wyrm's Crossing: A bridge so crowded you'd pay to cross without hearing a sales pitch! Traverse it only if you have to.

Gray Harbor

The trade the harbor brings in runs the city more than any single patriar. Coin is king, and morals are a jester frequently booed off stage. Harborhands jostle with pirates for space, treasure, and the best seafood stew (try the Low Lantern's). Bargain wisely, or you may prefer swimming with the fishes over facing the sharks on land.

Those windows have bars for a reason...

Anatomy of an ambush: a hooded man in blue, a woman with a baby. Can you spot the pickpocket?

Patriars refusing to disguise their telltale gait

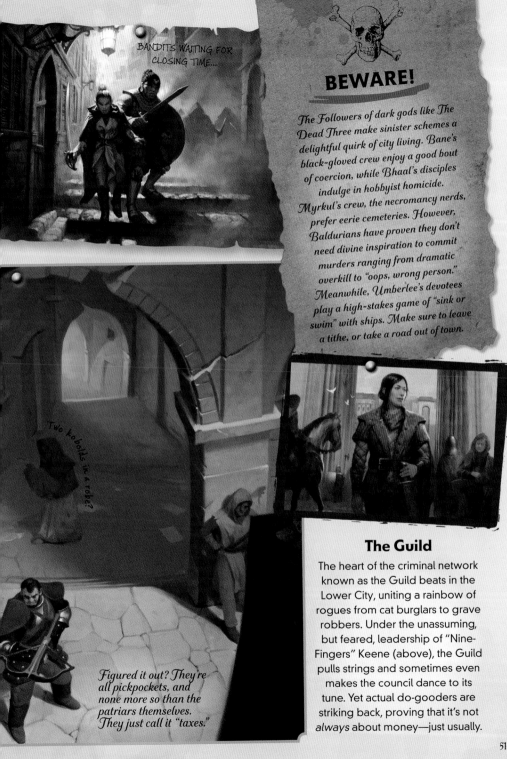

BANDITS WAITING FOR CLOSING TIME...

Two kobolds in a robe?

Figured it out? They're all pickpockets, and none more so than the patriars themselves. They just call it "taxes."

BEWARE!

The Followers of dark gods like The Dead Three make sinister schemes a delightful quirk of city living. Bane's black-gloved crew enjoy a good bout of coercion, while Bhaal's disciples indulge in hobbyist homicide. Myrkul's crew, the necromancy nerds, prefer eerie cemeteries. However, Baldurians have proven they don't need divine inspiration to commit murders ranging from dramatic overkill to "oops, wrong person." Meanwhile, Umberlee's devotees play a high-stakes game of "sink or swim" with ships. Make sure to leave a tithe, or take a road out of town.

The Guild

The heart of the criminal network known as the Guild beats in the Lower City, uniting a rainbow of rogues from cat burglars to grave robbers. Under the unassuming, but feared, leadership of "Nine-Fingers" Keene (above), the Guild pulls strings and sometimes even makes the council dance to its tune. Yet actual do-gooders are striking back, proving that it's not *always* about money—just usually.

51

BALDUR'S GATE: DAY TRIPS

(IF YOU'RE LIBERAL ABOUT WHAT CONSTITUTES A DAY)

North toward the Troll Hills, ogres debate the finer points of "club diplomacy." South to Cloakwood, trees gossip and druids fuss over foliage. Trek east for kobolds pestering travelers and setting snares. Westward? Pirates! Alas, they're all at sea with their sense of direction. From Baldur's Gate, you can't go right!

Nestled on the Sword Coast looms Candlekeep, hoarding lore where sea spray meets scholar's squabble.

Candlekeep from the southeast

Gain entry by presenting a tome, the more obscure the better, to appease the gatewarden.

Seagulls flee Candlekeep's spires, perhaps spooked by the library's ghostly silver dragon.

Candlekeep

Candlekeep is a literal fortress of knowledge, towering with tomes. Here, monks ponder over parchments and sages squabble over a single scroll for days. The books are so revered that a sneeze near the stacks might just get you exiled to the Outer Planes.

Watch for signs!

TRAVEL ON THE COAST WAY

1
There is safety in numbers, so form an adventuring party with a crew you trust. Keep your wits about you as you may cross staffs with a stubborn troll who's forgotten which bridge he's supposed to guard.

2
Midway, rest at wayfarer inns where the stew is questionable but the rumors are golden. Camping in the open with so many cut-throats in the vicinity is pretty much asking to be robbed.

3
A journey's end is rich with tales—minotaur ballads, wizardry gone awry. Each traveler's yarn spins into the tapestry of the Coast Way's legend. Some even make their living from it.

Poring over the greatest tomes in existence: Volo's Guides. Probably.

Durlag's Tower

A stone sentinel against the skyline, a dungeon delver's delight! Built by a dwarf with a paranoia surplus, Durlag's Tower presents a maze of puzzles where the walls have trust issues. Tread lightly—unless you want to dance with doppelgangers or parley with petrification. Seek its treasures, but leave breadcrumbs; the exit proves as elusive as a displacer beast.

For further adventures, set sail—swift tides avoid the highway's many-footed menaces. South, the mercantile nation of Amn awaits, with its bustling markets and arcane wonders.

WATERDEEP

CITY OF SPLENDORS
(AND A FEW TOO MANY STATUES)

Entering Waterdeep makes a new adventurer's jaw drop faster than a rogue's clumsy attempt at stealth. Amidst its towering walls and bustling streets, no one cares if you're different as long as you're paying for that pie you've been eyeing. It's a dream come true—if you can afford it.

How did Waterdeep become so splendid? Some credit Open Lord Laeral Silverhand's radiance. Others point to deep magic, the guilds' deeper pockets, and the excessively large dungeon that lies deeper still: Undermountain. Regardless, the Masked Lords had little hand in it, preferring anonymous governance to doing anything useful.

Some might be dazzled by the Castle District, giant statues, and flying griffons—personally I find it all a bit over the top...

The "Honorable Knight" walking statue

Volo in his natural habitat spins tales taller than a storm giant, yet somehow pulls you in. Every. Single. Time.

Yes, visit the famed Yawning Portal Inn, but avoid talking to Volo at all costs unless you WANT him to rope you into following him around all of Faerûn. Maybe that's just me.

Rainrun Street, home to the aforementioned Yawning Portal Inn. Tell Durnan the barkeep that I sent you.

KEY LOCATIONS

Castle Ward Besides the Open and Masked Lords of the "government," Blackstaff Tower looms, where the city's Archmage likely conjures more than just spells.

City of the Dead A graveyard so exclusive even the ghosts brag about residing in the upmarket section.

Dock Ward Waterdeep's bustling harbor hub, a maze of winding streets where the deals are as shady as the alleyways.

Sea Ward Upscale residents count their riches, then visit the Field of Triumph stadium to root for the underdog.

Keep any magic under wraps—too impressive and you'll have the Watch watching you. The shiny Guard defend the city, while the Navy's busy being unsinkable and the Griffon Cavalry are showing off. Bear in mind that Waterdeep's nobles view new money like a cat views a bath—necessary, but highly uncomfortable. Rich adventurers might buy mansions, but they can't buy centuries of noble snootiness.

Between "The Sahuagin Humbled" and "The Great Drunkard" (pictured), the city's giant, formerly mobile statues are now just targets for griffon droppings. Still, worth keeping an eye on them— they could cause havoc if they were to suddenly spring back to life.

The decrepit Skewered Dragon in the Docks hosts gambling—and the odd ambush by Zhentarim agents.

WATERDEEP: FESTIVALS

BECAUSE EVERY DAY THEY FIND A REASON TO CELEBRATE, APPARENTLY

Festivals pop up like eager goblins spotting shiny loot. Enjoy the masked antics of Liar's Night or drink yourself under your own table during Midsummer. Not all is merriment: you may be forced to remember your departed aunt's snaggletooth as you honor the ancestors in the Feast of the Moon. (Waterdhavians really will take any excuse for a day off.)

KEY INFO

Find a parade route: Track the telltale signs, such as streets freshly swept, guards in particularly shiny armor, and townsfolk donning peculiar hats or suddenly bursting into song.

Stock up: Have bread, cheese, and a flask of ale, so an epidemic of closed shops doesn't leave you the only one without a snack!

Trolltide and Day of Wonders

Two holidays, endless mischief. Trolltide sees kids and the occasional band of goblins mimic trolls for treats, while the Day of Wonders honors the innovations of Gond, god of craft, with mechanical marvels parading. Fair warning: it's not unusual for rogue cogs to trip people up. Celebrate, but watch your toes!

A FESTIVE, LOVED-UP FOOL

BEWARE!

Amid Waterdeep's myriad celebrations lurk darker festivities honoring gods like Shar, goddess of darkness, or Malar, god of hunting (and savagery). Always double-check your gala invitation; it might not be the kind of party a young adventurer would hope for. You could end up with a cursed conch forever whispering chilling prayers to Umberlee, goddess of the sea, ensuring you never sleep peacefully again. For example. Worse yet, even benign celebrations can prove a tempting target for nefarious plots. Party with all eyes open!

The Watchful Order (Waterdeep's wizards' guild) might just crash your new romance if they think charm spells and alcohol have been mixed!

YOU'LL NEED ONE OF THESE!

MIDSUMMER NIGHT'S REVEL STEP-BY-STEP

1

Slip into your most eyebrow-raising ensemble, channeling "tipsy wizard at a masquerade." Forget your attire? Raid a bard's closet. They won't notice—they're already three sheets to the wind.

2

With doors flung wide as invites, and desserts served atop the daring, partake in Waterdeep's risqué games and laughter. By dawn, aim for "I did WHAT?" levels of amnesia!

3

As you swirl in moonlit dances, remember: that fourth goblet of mead might have you pledging love to a random gnome. Sure, a curative spell will sober you up, but it won't un-betroth you to that pie merchant!

Midwinter's Toast

Raising goblets high, join the nobles as they renew their alliances. Or if you're a commoner? It's the "thank the gods we're halfway through winter" feast, and then right back to work...

Midsummer Revel: 1, Adventurer: 0. Don't miss out on the fun. Pace yourself so you can last till morning!

57

WATERDEEP: SKULLPORT

THE DARKER DEPTHS (OR THE BEST PLACE TO BUY SKULL-THEMED SOUVENIRS)

Beneath Waterdeep lies a market of mystery. It suppresses magic, but not good times. Beholders bargain, drow dicker, and adventurers? They're trying not to lose more than just their money! It's the Port of Shadow—where the only thing darker than the alleys might be the deals. Browse at your own risk!

KEY INFO

There are a few different ways to get to Skullport.

The Undermountain River Sargauth: Delve into a submerged route boasting the smell of the many, many who have gone before you and a constant ambient dampness.

Meandering Undermountain tunnels: Choose from five unique tunnels—from the melodramatic echoes of Whisperhaunt to Beggar's Rest's quirky goblin hospitality.

The sea caves: A maritime challenge with treacherous waves, shipwrecks, and aquatic locals. Beware the broken hoist. Some have tried *mending* spells—results vary.

Skullport as seen from Skull Island: a view only a beholder could love.

Bring your own elf or bring your own torch, because light is not complimentary. Unless you count the flameskulls.

At street level, "neighbors" means "our buildings are literally on top of each other."

Not a torch!

Ancient flameskulls rule Skullport, stuck in a nostalgic loop, laughing and babbling in dead tongues.

A Night on the Town

Since you've chosen to visit Skullport and therefore may not have long to live, why not indulge in an evening of fun—or day, really, for who knows what time it is here. Visit a pawnshop for rare finds, quench your thirst at the Flagon and Dragon, place bets at the Bat's Roost fighting den, or adopt a critter from the Feathered Rat!

BEWARE!

Surviving Skullport requires more than dodging flameskulls. Murkspan Bridge's sudden drop feature offers surprise swimming lessons, while Skull Island's ship-gobbling harbors greet sailors with a fatal embrace. Beware of the ever-watchful sea hags—peeping toms of the nautical underworld. Worse, assume everyone is on the Xanathar's payroll. Why? Because he would never act on his own. And with all his resources, his so-called "Guide to Everything" is a full 33 pages shorter than Volo's! Where are the skyejotuns? The tlincalli? "Volo's Guide to Monsters" has them. Do you know how hard it was for Volo to trudge through the swamps all by himself for the froghemoths? He won't admit it, but I can tell. The Xanathar doesn't have a fraction of Volo's courage. "Guide to Everything," my left horn.

The Xanathar

The eye-rolling ruling beholder of Skullport's underbelly. Obsessed with treasures, trinkets, and his beloved goldfish, Sylgar, he supposedly penned *Xanathar's Guide* —probably to copy Volo's. My guess? He had his guild do the legwork for him! Claims to control the underworld, but his management style? Questionable. Rumor has it, even Sylgar thinks it could lead better.

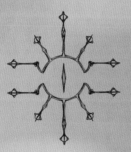

Xanathar guild symbols

Guild members know zero about the Xanathar. They can't even spot the beholder vibes in their own emblem!

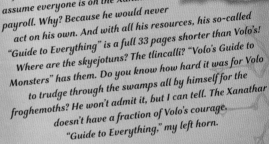

SKULLPORT DINING

The Black Tankard: Ever tried the Wyrmwizz? Tastes just like... well, dirt. Best dirt cheap dirt you'll ever have, promise!

The Worm's Gullet: Ever pondered dining inside a giant worm? Ponder no longer! Gharz Stonedark's unique "chef's surprise" approach ensures you'll never get the same meal twice (or even know what you're eating).

The Flagon and the Dragon: With Cal'al's ever-cheery greeting of "What's your poison?", she's either hinting at the tavern's extensive drink menu or suggesting she knows a lot more about potions than you might think.

WATERDEEP: UNDERMOUNTAIN

THE LABYRINTHINE DUNGEON OUT TO PROVE IT'S MORE THAN JUST WATERDEEP'S BASEMENT

This, the original mega-dungeon, sprawls beneath Waterdeep's streets, offering great rewards and greater perils. Secret doors outnumber rats, and the echoes might just talk back. Master its endless mazes and unexpected pit stops for that rarest of treasures: escaping back to the tavern above for a well-earned ale. Perfect for adventurers who thought, "What I really need in life is more dark corridors."

warily respectful) feet.

Many go down... few come back up.

The Yawning Portal Inn is Waterdeep's gateway to Undermountain. Drop into its well for an adventure after a few too many, then climb out with stories for Volo to steal.

BEWARE!

Undermountain takes "trap" to heart. Lean on a wall, find yourself skewered by darts that won't quit until they've emptied their arsenal. Step on a tile, fall twenty feet. Lucky for you, some traps sulk for an hour before being ready for round two. It's a lesson in trust: here, even the architecture holds a grudge.

Also loves blast scepters!

Halaster Blackcloak: Undermountain's insane architect, proving even wizards need hobbies—his just involve creating murderous dungeons to perplex adventurers.

60

MONTICORES

RUST MONSTERS

SEA HAGS

CHUULS

DISPLACER BEASTS

UMBER HULKS

STONE GIANTS

BULLYWUGS

DO / DO NOT

- **DO** show respect to any resident drow matrons as you inch toward the door. Manners won't kill you, but they probably will.

- **DO** compliment a mind flayer's intellect. It might consider sparing your brain... until later.

- <u>DO NOT</u> attempt to pet any displacer beasts. They're not where you think they are.

- <u>DO NOT</u> aim to visit all of Undermountain's levels in one go. You will run out of supplies, and you will not like your dining options.

Undermountain's Perils

Halaster loves to reshuffle the dungeon's layout, making getting lost your only guarantee. And let's not forget its entrance to the Underdark, a gateway to even greater terrors beneath. And the fiendish traps. Plus, monsters. Lots and lots of monsters. Better take *Volo's Guide* with you!

DROW

TROGLODYTES

FIRE GIANTS

PURPLE WORMS

Other Nasties

Hungry, slimy, often corrosive creatures are the workforce of any dungeon, and Undermountain is no exception. Gelatinous cubes, oozes, and their ilk have forced adventurers to look up, down, and all around since time immemorial. Beware any suspiciously corpse-free areas; something has been eating them.

Gelatinous cube

Mimics

Yellow ochre

Gray ooze

A PARTY OF FOOLS BRAVE THE PERILS OF UNDERMOUNTAIN...

Between the Moonwood's lycanthropes and the Rauvin Mountains' impressive peaks, there's never a dull (or entirely safe) hiking trip in the Silver Marches!

THE SILVER MARCHES

WHERE ELVES, DWARVES, AND HUMANS PLAY NICE (MOSTLY)

Also called Luruar, this former confederation of cities feels like a set of mismatched fabrics stitched together into a surprisingly fetching set of robes. Anchored by Silverymoon, the "Bard College Town of the North," it's a place of song, magic, and the occasional diplomatic incident over beard lengths.

With Lady Alustriel once head of its magic school, the city of Silverymoon shines as a beacon of... well, shiny things, usually conjured. Leave the mundane behind by crossing the enchanting Moonbridge and spot a mage conversing earnestly with one of their many illusions. The Marches? Think of it as a frontier where nature's splendor meets "Is that elf looking at me funny?", with the occasional orc invasion thrown in.

SILVERYMOON: DO / DO NOT

- **DO** cross the delightful Moon Bridge.
- **DO NOT** flaunt your latest fire spell; the bridge's protective mythal force won't like it.
- **DO NOT** attack anyone on it, or the bridge might blink out of existence!
- **DO** pretend you were yawning instead.
- **DO** browse the vast knowledge within the Vault of the Sages.

WAR ZONE SURVIVAL TIPS

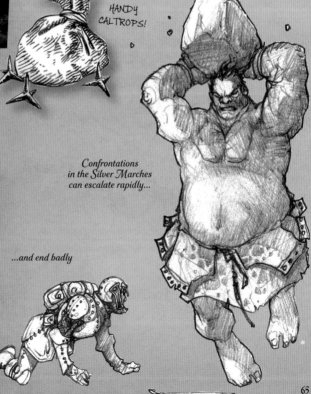

Ballista Bonus

Always position your ballista with the view of a scenic horizon. If it's going to take an age to reload, at least you can enjoy the picturesque scenery while waiting.

Dwarven Camouflage

Befriend a dwarf, and when things get hectic, hide behind their majestic beard. Plus, it's surprisingly cozy under there!

Orcish Language Classes

While some grunts and snarls might sound similar, nuances matter. Study up, and you could avoid unfortunate misunderstandings. Like, say, mistaking a war cry for a dinner invite.

The literal best place to hide during an orc raid: inside a burning ruin.

The detritus of a recent orc invasion, marking the unceremonious dissolution of the Silver Marches (They have cleaned up since then).

With their high walls, the cities of the Silver Marches can feel unwelcoming. But don't miss the chance to visit the old dwarven Citadel Felbarr, which abandoned its exclusive "no-humans-allowed" card gatherings centuries ago. And if you believe only mines await in Mithral Hall, you'll miss out on the famed hospitality of the dwarves of Clan Battlehammer, bewildered goblins stumbling into traps, ancient relics, and... lots of lovely rocks.

HANDY CALTROPS!

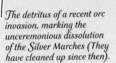

Confrontations in the Silver Marches can escalate rapidly...

...and end badly

LUSKAN

THE CITY OF SAILS—AND SURPRISINGLY AMBITIOUS PIRATES

Here, pirate captains rule as unofficial mayors, and town meetings devolve into deck-swabbing disputes. Meanwhile, the Arcane Brotherhood's footprint proves impossible to ignore. With someone always staking a claim to something, the whole city is a harbor brawl waiting to happen.

One doesn't cross any old bridge in Luskan. Be prepared for a complex dance of who-can-walk-where without getting a scolding. The sinister wizards of the Arcane Brotherhood can be identified by their fancy cloaks and claim that they're neutral and "just here for the magic." Volo couldn't stop laughing at that one... Wherever you go in Luskan, keep an eye on your coin, and your hand on some kind of weapon.

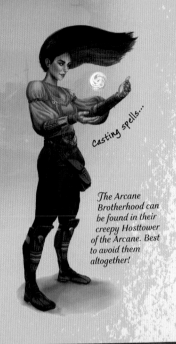

Casting spells...

The Arcane Brotherhood can be found in their creepy Hosttower of the Arcane. Best to avoid them altogether!

The Hosttower of the Arcane apparently decided to sprout five spires and overshadow Luskan's skyline on its own!

Bregan D'aerthe

These drow elf mercenaries moonlight as Luskan's unofficial nightlife managers. If something's amiss at midnight, they probably scheduled it. The job isn't done until the gold's counted and the shadows are checked twice.

...and breaking hearts.

Bregan D'aerthe's leader Jarlaxle Baenre cuts a dashing figure— and any who cross him.

THE SHIPS

Not actual floating vessels, the gangs known as the Ships dominate Luskan's politics with fierce rivalry. While Ship Kurth handles the docks, looking smug with its plethora of vessels, poor Ship Rethnor is left guarding dirty alleys and hoping for a coin or two. The others are Baram (in charge of fishing), Taerl (any jobs going) and Suljack (raiders extraordinaire). No fancy cloaks for these pirates, because nothing says Ship loyalty like a facial tattoo. Wander carelessly into their waters and you might just stumble upon a spirited debate... or an impromptu swimming lesson.

HARBOR HORRORS

- DO bow before a dragon turtle before fleeing; it's considered good sea etiquette.

- DO quickly bandage any injuries; sahuagin are driven into a frenzy by the smell of fresh blood.

- DO NOT ask a kraken for directions; they're bad at it.

- DO NOT get too close to a sea hag; they're so hideous just looking at one can strike fear into even the bravest adventurers.

A view of Luskan from the west

PIRATE FROM SHIP KURTH DEFINITELY SULJACK!

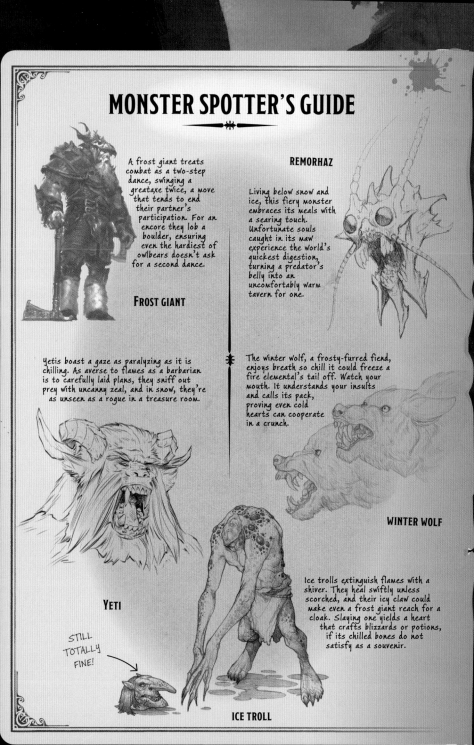

MONSTER SPOTTER'S GUIDE

A frost giant treats combat as a two-step dance, swinging a greataxe twice, a move that tends to end their partner's participation. For an encore they lob a boulder, ensuring even the hardiest of owlbears doesn't ask for a second dance.

FROST GIANT

REMORHAZ

Living below snow and ice, this fiery monster embraces its meals with a searing touch. Unfortunate souls caught in its maw experience the world's quickest digestion, turning a predator's belly into an uncomfortably warm tavern for one.

Yetis boast a gaze as paralyzing as it is chilling. As averse to flames as a barbarian is to carefully laid plans, they sniff out prey with uncanny zeal, and in snow, they're as unseen as a rogue in a treasure room.

The winter wolf, a frosty-furred fiend, enjoys breath so chill it could freeze a fire elemental's tail off. Watch your mouth. It understands your insults and calls its pack, proving even cold hearts can cooperate in a crunch.

WINTER WOLF

YETI

Ice trolls extinguish flames with a shiver. They heal swiftly unless scorched, and their icy claw could make even a frost giant reach for a cloak. Slaying one yields a heart that crafts blizzards or potions, if its chilled bones do not satisfy as a souvenir.

STILL TOTALLY FINE!

ICE TROLL

CHAPTER 3.
THE FROZENFAR

ICEWIND DALE

A COLD SO ENDURING EVEN THE ICE ELEMENTALS WEAR JACKETS

This northern frontier, nestled between the Spine of the World mountains and the Sea of Moving Ice, offers more than just the Ten-Towns. The cruel goddess Auril's chill ensures every breath turns to mist, though the locals consider the auroras the best show you'll ever shiver through.

> When sailing the Sea of Moving Ice, watch out for icebergs. That's it. That's all the advice. The clue's in the name.

Life here is cold, hard, and unforgiving, and the locals do what they must to survive. Which for goblins means zipping around on wolves, ambushing travelers with all the grace of a drunken ogre on ice skates, while the Reghed barbarians roam with the reindeer like they're part of the herd.

The heroic barbarian Wulfgar, Icewind Dale's unofficial ambassador (of smashing), offers a unique blend of diplomacy and

Not every creature in Icewind Dale wants to eat you. Some just want to show off their fancy antlers...

...or fall on top of your little boat and crush you into little bits.

I'D STICK WITH SLED DOGS!

If you want to get around, you're going to need sled dogs. Or if you're feeling bold, use the goblins' idea: polar bears.

DO / DO NOT

- **DO** try the local knucklehead trout. It's the only fish that doubles as both a dinner and a bludgeoning weapon.

- **DO** challenge a frost giant to a snowball fight; they've got a mean throw but a slow dodge.

- **DO NOT** mess with the wildlife. To live here, animals have to be big, bad, and extremely hard to kill.

hammer therapy, quite literally. When he speaks, even frost giants listen... or get a close-up of his hammer, Aegis-fang! Then there's Arveiaturace, the nearsighted white dragon. She stashes her hoard in a pirate ship, seemingly confusing "plundering" with "decorating." Flying with her wizard master's stone-dead body still on her back, she redefines "holding onto your past" in the most literal, frostbitten way possible.

KEY LOCATIONS

Callidae A sub-glacial city home to a secret (oops) enclave of aevendrow—elves so cool they make the ice jealous.

Kelvin's Cairn A towering, snow-capped mountain where dwarves of Clan Battlehammer mine beneath the ice, probably trying to find a warmer climate.

Revel's End Controlled by the Lords' Alliance, this frosty fortress houses those who've been especially naughty. Visitors are extremely unwelcome.

Reghed Glacier A massive ice wall that hides a bubbling spring. Ideal for a chilly slide, if you dare.

The Lakes Maer Dualdon, Redwaters, and Lac Dinneshere. Three lakes that offer the finest fishing this side of the Spine of the World. Just don't fall in, because I guarantee no one is coming in after you.

TEN-TOWNS

BECAUSE ELEVEN WOULD JUST BE SHOWING OFF

Outcasts find their people in these hamlets, because survival's a group project in the art of not freezing. These modest trading posts grew into a federation around lakes that only semi-freeze, thanks to nature's under-lake heating. Here, warmth is the currency and a smile from a bundled-up neighbor is worth its weight in firewood.

Thieves once swiped the lantern, but not the charm, at the Northern Light Inn in Caer-Konig. Here, the innkeeps' sisterly squabbles are the main entertainment.

Trust me, it looks much nicer from a distance!

Lac Dinneshere is full of fish (and careless adventurers).

Ten-Towns' Top Taverns

Only ten towns but tons of taverns (probably because there isn't much else to do). The Buried Treasures shines in Bremen, where innkeep Cora treats treasure-seekers like they've struck gold. The Uphill Climb in Caer-Dineval boasts lake views that almost make up for its lack of spirits. And why enjoy safety in Bryn Shander when you can enjoy dodging Ol' Bitey at the rowdy Northlook?

KEY INFO

Keep warm: Far from the forests, that means burning whale oil or hugging your neighbor. Whale oil lamps provide a cozy, if slightly fishy, ambiance.

Avoid flashy spells: Magic is scarcer than a warm day to these folks. The local magician more likely sells candles than summons fire elementals.

Find transportation: Hire an axe beak, the feathered, snow-striding, toe-splaying wonders of the tundra. Dogsleds are the wagons of the north, so tip your canine driver with a nice bone.

PERIODICALLY COMES ALIVE

In Easthaven, growth and reinvention are the norms, and honoring the town's thieving founders means legalized light-fingered larceny. Watch your belongings, or they'll walk!

Dealing with the Locals

The chances of locals consigning you to the flames are slim, but never zero. As long as you're not a murderous wizard and you avoid winning (losing?) the sacrificial lottery to Auril, the locals are friendly enough, like walking, grumbling snowmen with strong opinions on fishing.

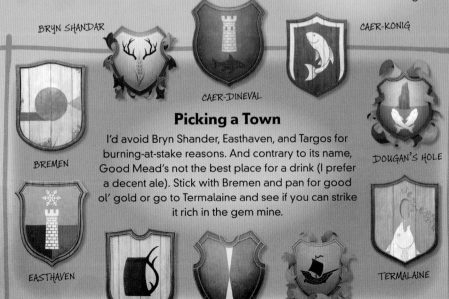

BRYN SHANDAR

CAER-KONIG

CAER-DINEVAL

BREMEN

DOUGAN'S HOLE

Picking a Town

I'd avoid Bryn Shander, Easthaven, and Targos for burning-at-stake reasons. And contrary to its name, Good Mead's not the best place for a drink (I prefer a decent ale). Stick with Bremen and pan for good ol' gold or go to Termalaine and see if you can strike it rich in the gem mine.

EASTHAVEN

TERMALAINE

GOOD MEAD

LONELYWOOD

TARGOS

COLD WEATHER SURVIVAL

WHEN YOU HAVEN'T THE SENSE TO STAY SOMEPLACE WARM

From the Utter East to the Spine of the World, even a barbarian's beard can freeze! Pack extra socks, dance nightly with fire spells, and cuddle your warlock. Worst case, burn *"Xanathar's Guide"* for warmth. Or where Volo's concerned, spite.

Fur-trimmed gloves: nature's way of saying "Who needs magic when you've got cozy fingers?"

HARPOONS OPTIONAL

Look at them, laughing at winter.

Take sartorial inspiration from these Reghed tribespeople–it could save your life!

IT'S EASIER IF THE WOLF IS ALREADY DEAD

A well-constructed shelter of pelts could mean the difference between waking up cold and waking up dead.

Cold Weather Gear

A hero's journey in blistering cold demands insulated tunics, extra-warm mittens, stout boots, and dramatic cloaks that shout "Winter, I laugh at thee!" Don't miss a step: strap on your snowshoes or crampons to brave snow and ice without plummeting through it.

FINDING FOOD

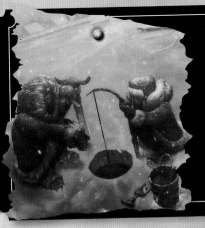

1

In the wintry wilds, scout for nuts, seeds, and the occasional misfit berry. Think of them as Faerûn's little energy pouches handed out by a truly neutral druid! Ice fishing is also an option, but beware—more than just fish lurk beneath the ice.

2

Hone your snaring skills: It's like wizardry, but less flashy and more fuzzy. Secure a well-fed rabbit or, on an odd day, perhaps a befuddled chicken pondering its poor life choices and questionable sense of direction. Always remember, nature's buffet is both bountiful and sometimes bewildered!

KEY INFO

Melt it down: When tempted by an icy brook, always remember the legendary advice whispered in mead halls—melt first, guzzle second. A drink's more rewarding when it's not been chipped from the stream!

No Sweat: When it comes to clothing, aim for "snug ranger" not "steamy troll." Too many layers and you'll start sweating, which spells a chilly disaster in waiting! Balance is key!

BEWARE!

Auril, the Frostmaiden, loves her jests and whiteout blizzards that thwart even the twilight-sighted. A chill up your spine could be your chain mail's inherent draftiness, or it could be an ice sprite... When that biting cold won't quit, snuggle in a snow hut or nestle beneath a sturdy pine—without letting virgin snow trick you into falling down a tree well. Finally, if the urge to strip down or nap with a yeti hits, and (unlike me) you can't breathe fire, get thee in front of one, posthaste!

Lost in the Wastes?

So you didn't bring a ranger on your icy adventure. Big mistake. Not as big a mistake as challenging a frost giant to a duel, but still. Don't compound that mistake by testing your luck with wild wanderings. Find a spot, make it yours, and maybe construct a defensive snow fortress. Send up a flare with a minor spell, and hope someone heeds the call. Frostbite? Not a fun souvenir. Warm up, await rescue, and don't fret. Every misadventure you survive makes a grand tavern tale later!

SOME WARMING MEAD WILL PUT THE "PARTY" IN RESCUE PARTY

CREATURES OF THE COLD

IF IT'S FLUFFY, MAYBE DON'T LIE ON IT

In the midst of freezing in a snowstorm, you lock eyes with a white, furry monstrosity. That brave-the-cold plan doesn't seem quite so brilliant now, does it? Have no fear (and no warmth). Herein lies how to out-chill the chill and outsmart the fluff!

Not a friendly hug...

...it's a trap!

With a freezing gaze and bear hugs that are literally bone-crushing, better to admire yetis from a safe distance, like from Waterdeep.

Crafted from dark magical crystals, this dragon construct radiates malevolence, spreading more terror than a bard's off-key ballad at a packed tavern.

Gird yourself for encounters on land, sea, air, and undersnow if you choose to head out into the Frozen North. I would not.

Remorhazes run hot and cold. Cold when lying in wait under the snow, and blazing hot when trying to eat you. Simple.

At least you'll die warm.

Maer Dualdon's lake monster: maybe a lizard improbably surviving in frigid temperatures, maybe not, but definitely a fan of the local boat-based cuisine.

Snowy owlbears: like their forest cousins, these majestic creatures are a blend of hoot and roar! Just remember, they might look cuddly, but those talons aren't for show.

BURN IT OR IT RETURNS! ⟶

An ice troll's aura snuffs out flames, but its heart makes a nifty blizzard-maker.

Planning a tranquil walk in Lonelywood? Prepare for more than frosty breath. Winter wolves have been known to challenge visitors to a game of freeze-tag. They always win.

BEWARE!

Sure, fear the frost giants, but beware the small fry too. Ice mephits are jagged little elemental nasties that can turn an evening into a very bad time. They even explode in a shower of razor-sharp ice if you kill them. Worse still are the bheur hags—Auril's handmaidens. Creepy blue-skinned nightmares that would just love to eat your freshly frozen corpse.

COLD ENCOUNTERS STEP-BY-STEP

1

Squint hard. That mound of snow might just be a dozing yeti. If it snores, step away from the monster.

2

Ditch those ice spells; they're about as useful as an empty wand. Arm yourself with fire, or a fiery dragonborn (who I guarantee will not be having a good time in the snow.)

3

If you defeat your foe, turn its pelt into your next Cloak of Natural Warmth. Wear it as a trophy and a testament to your survival skills. Who said you can't be both practical and intimidating?

MONSTER SPOTTER'S GUIDE

Ceiling dwellers and savvy diners, grell patiently wait for you to finish your battle before surprising you with a nice dinner—and you're the main course. Always hungry, occasionally shocking.

GRELL

Really nasty brain-eaters. Can levitate and control the minds of others. Have cold, rubbery skin and tentacles. Avoid at all costs!

MIND FLAYER

Walking mushrooms who put the "fun" in fungi. Not really... they're actually pretty placid. They like spores. A LOT. Try not to breathe them in.

A flying leather cloak that bites hard. Can't handle bright lights. Loves lurking and making illusory buddies to hang out with instead of real ones. Its moan is scarier than Volo's singing.

CLOAKER

MYCONID

Vulture head, beetle bod, big on hooky arms. Talks with clacks that echo everywhere. Cliffhanger pro, ambushes from above. Hunts in packs, but sore losers. They flee and sulk.

This sneaky stone mimic acts like a stalagmite, but with tendrils and a gnarly bite. Climbs upside down, loves a feast, but finds gems indigestible. Grab its leftovers, if you survive.

HOOK HORROR

ROPER

Friendly telepathic brainiac. Nibbles on psionic energy. Spills secrets if you're good. Glows pink when amused, blue when sad, and red when you poke it with a stick.

FLUMPH

DON'T DO THIS!

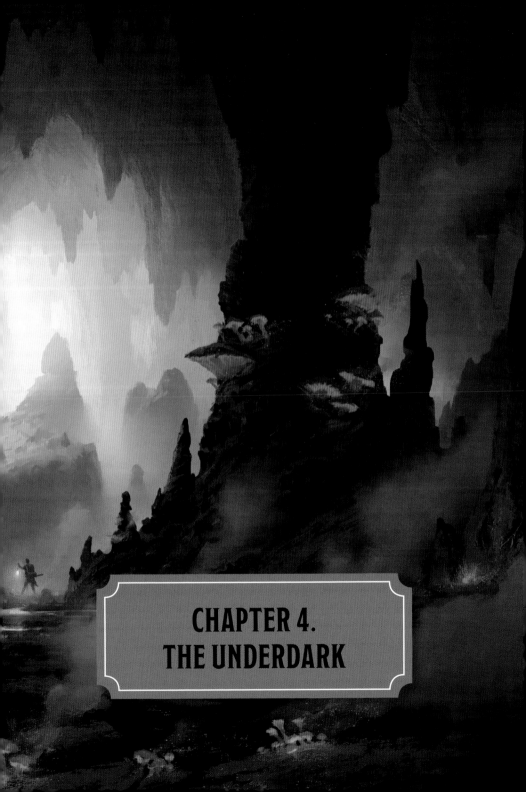

CHAPTER 4.
THE UNDERDARK

LOCATION

In the Underdark, glowing mushrooms and critters are your nightlights, saving you from stubbing your toe on a stalagmite—or a sleeping umber hulk.

If scaling Underdark walls, watch for mushrooms. Some scream, some explode, others make you think you're in love with, say, Volo. For example.

THE UNDERDARK

LIKE YOUR BASEMENT, BUT BIGGER— AND WITH MORE MONSTERS

This vast subterranean labyrinth consists of twisted tunnels and colossal caverns where the stalactites may just be the second most dangerous thing that could drop on an unwary traveler's head. The first? Take your pick. Here light is precious, echoes mislead, and the paths have a pesky habit of shifting behind you like they have a mind of their own.

In these shadowy mazes, a friendly face is one that isn't currently eating you, and power plays out in a treacherous dance of deceit. The spider-loving udadrow, led by "noble" Houses that would sooner backstab than bow, vie for power. Drizzt Do'Urden, famed renegade of Menzoberranzan, defies these dark norms with an actual moral compass. Meanwhile, dour duergar dwarves and secretive deep gnomes compete for resources, and mind flayers exert psychic domination. Trust is as scarce as daylight here, where the enemy of your enemy... is just another enemy biding their time.

KEY LOCATIONS

Menzoberranzan
A subterranean udadrow nexus venerating spider queen Lolth; rife with duplicity, clandestine machinations, fungal cuisine, and spider silk bridges, all under the sinister glow of arcane lights.

Darklake An accurately named body of water. Here, evading the udadrow means teaming with fishlike kuo-toa guides, and a well-paddled mushroom-cap coracle could be your only ticket to survival.

Oryndoll Add this grimly silent but psionically buzzing mind flayer city to your list of must-nevers. Not even the duergar want to visit, and they were created there.

Blingdenstone This city bustles with gem trading, though negotiating with its deep gnome inhabitants can be a rocky experience!

DO / DO NOT

- **DO** don a helm of darkvision, lest you mistake a hook horror for your party mate.
- **DO NOT** snack on random fungi; the Underdark isn't your personal larder, and their spores could easily make you their servant.
- **DO** tip your deep gnome guide, unless you actually want a "shortcut" through a purple worm's dining hall.

Menzoberranzan's spires are draped in spider silk that masquerades as snow— perhaps the real reason Drizzt preferred cold feet to eight-legged deceit.

If you can get one, an udadrow piwafwi cloak will help you hide from subterranean terrors.

NAVIGATING THE DARKNESS

LEFT AT THE GIANT SPIDER, RIGHT AT THE CREEPY ECHOING...

The Underdark wants you. Really. Pitfalls and bottomless pits love company. For a surefire trick to attract every creature in the dark, ring their dinner bell by wearing jangling armor. And no, not every rock is a disguised mimic, but why risk it? If that wasn't enough, visitors must face all these perils under the influence of the *faerzress*, a magical radiation that serves as ambiance creator, divination disruptor, teleport blocker, and occasional wild magic prankster.

Setting up Camp

Look and listen. If you hear a hook horror's chorus of clicking, don't camp; you won't get any rest! Always aim for places without skeletons. If that's not possible, the fewer skeletons, the better. Otherwise you might have to flee mid-meal and abandon any precious leftovers. But hey, once your party has cleared an area, you can set up an outpost for your very own subterranean safe haven! Safe-ish.

Lighting Your Way

Torches work well, but anyone with a nose will smell you coming. Try a *continual flame* spell for a fancy candlelit dinner feel, or a *light* cantrip spell as your personal will-o'-the-wisp. What if you're the only one in the party with no darkvision? Goggles of Night ensure you see every creepy tunnel (although some things are better left unseen).

Subterranean Sustenance

Surface supplies will run out eventually. Dawdle down here long enough and you'll need to find food. If you're planning an extended stay (why?!) you could set up camp and start a mushroom farm, get creative with spells like *goodberry*, or learn to forage. Avoid day-old monster meat unless your stomach can flash-fry things. What about drow mushroom steaks? An exotic treat, if you can handle eating Ripplebark fungus that looks like rotting flesh.

The Wormwrithings

Think giant worm-made spaghetti. Throughout the Underdark, these tunnels intersect in a maze only a minotaur could love. A jaunt without a map will turn into a bewildering hike in circles, where every turn could lead to a kobold party (with you as the unwilling guest of honor), or a purple worm's unwelcome hello.

A portrait in denial: Adventurers search for proof a purple worm came through.

The Silken Paths: a giant spider's dream and your navigation nightmare. Fight the urge to burn it all down, because it's a long drop.

DENIZENS OF THE DARK

EVERYONE'S LOOKING FOR SOMETHING: SOME THINGS ARE LOOKING FOR YOU

Leave the sunlight behind and venture below to find a labyrinthine world of wonders and terrors. Home to udadrow, mind flayers, hook horrors, and stranger things still, it's like a bizarre family reunion, if your family had tentacles and plotted your demise over dinner.

KEY INFO

Light's Scarce, Wit's Abundant: The lack of light doesn't hinder the locals; they are darksighted like you wouldn't believe. For poor adventurers, torches are basically "I'm over here!" signs.

Trust's a Commodity: Friendliness is as rare as a sunbeam. Denizens here do trust like fire elementals do baths. Not very often. Flashing a smile? Suspicious. Flashing gold? Now we're talking.

Navigation is a Nightmare: With tunnels that twist like a politician's promise, a lost adventurer might become a permanent Underdark resident!

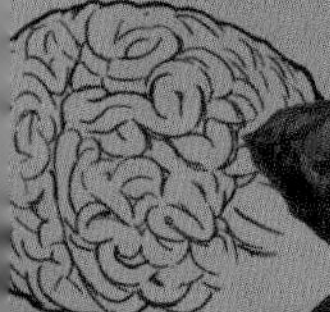

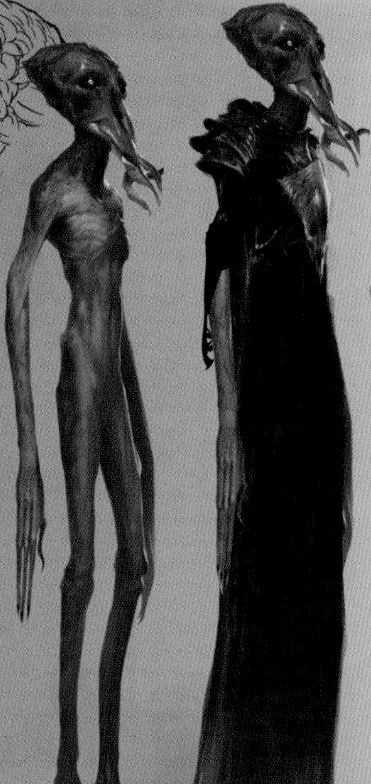

Ask not how it posed nude, but why.

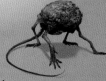

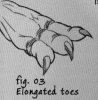

In battle, mind flayers unfurl long, clawed fingers to crack open a foe's skull for a quick, grisly brain feast.

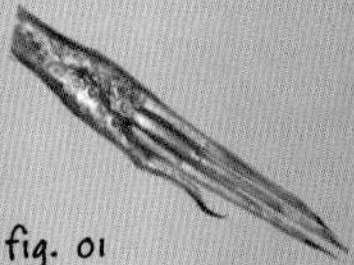

fig. 01
Talons

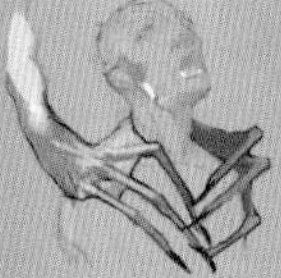

fig. 02
Death grasp

fig. 03
Elongated toes

Mind flayers

Mind flayers, with their noodly appendages and oversized brains, provide the universe's answer to "What if calamari fought back?" With psychic might they levitate and plunder thoughts at will, all to deliver the best possible meal to their colony's elder brain. Dinner is served, brains preferred.

Intellect devourers are mind flayer sidekicks. This brain on legs might just outsmart you before paralyzing you.

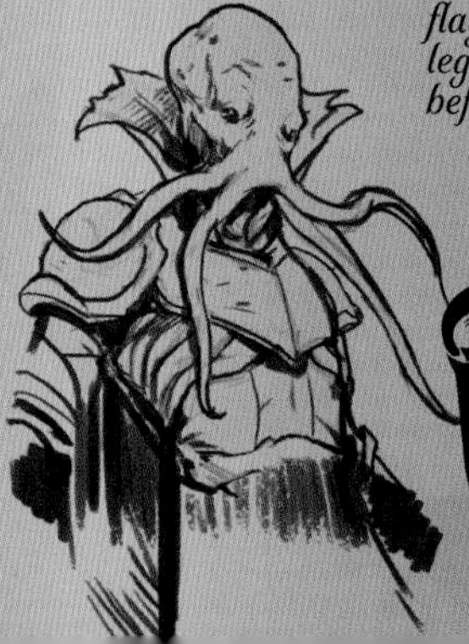

Mind flayers grapple with their slimy tentacles, stunning and reeling in prey like a nightmarish game of catch-and-never-release.

The udadrow: moody elves with a yen for dark caves. Many worship Lolth, the spider queen, united by a love of spiders and backstabbing.

fig. 01
Udadrow
shield with
(unsurprising)
spider motif

In the Underdark's rocky nooks, deep gnomes (svirfneblin) win as hide-and-seek champions, with gray skin for camouflage and a love of rubies that rivals their knack for evading unwelcome visitors.

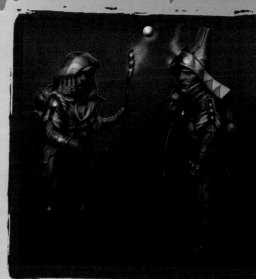

A duergar cavern explorer

Other Underdark Species

The Underdark does not belong to the udadrow and mind flayers alone. Duergar flex their gruffness, perfecting the art of the scowl. Myconids chatter through spore signals, making them the unspoken socialites of the caverns. Gentle flumphs float by, bestowing wisdom with a side of jellyfish elegance. With troglodytes' distinct odor and quaggoths' furry fury, it's clear the Underdark throws the most eclectic shindig in all the Realms.

EACH DUERGAR
BEARD TELLS A
TALE FORBIDDEN
TO OUTSIDERS

Grumbling gray dwarves, the duergar seek to expand their subterranean kingdoms. They can turn invisible and giant-sized at will, proving even the most tyrannical dwarf can throw a superb surprise party...

Myconids are not your average mushrooms. Sprouts are tiny telepaths; adults pack a punch with stunning spores; and the sovereigns, the grand shroom honchos, animate the dead. All share a dramatic flair for communal telepathy and a true distaste for sunny weather.

PERILS OF THE UNDERDARK

TRAVERSING THE DEPTHS WHERE MUSHROOMS GLOW BRIGHTER THAN YOUR FUTURE

It's so hard to pick the Underdark's worst. The udadrow? Sure, but they're not *all* bad... their spidersilk clothes are pretty slick. Whether running from mushrooms confused about the food chain, or running from your own shadow (or someone else's), you may likely also "enjoy" these subterranean challenges.

Confidently points ahead, oblivious to the robed cultists behind. Don't be this elf.

A shrine of the "Deep Father." AKA Demogorgon in disguise.

Weird Cults

Must be something about being undergound that attracts the crazies. The Cult of the Absolute, fanatical about their so-called true god, tend to clash with the Cult of BOOOAL's blood-thirsty fish folk. Pro tip: carry a fake pamphlet for each deity. That way they'll try to recruit each other, not you!

What you'll see about five seconds before Demogorgon rises...

Captured by Udadrow

Congratulations! You're the newest recruits for the udadrow's involuntary spa retreat, complete with tight iron jewelry and gourmet mushroom broth. Your daily exercise? Backbreaking labor, plotting to escape with fellow "guests," and hoping you don't end up on a one-way trip to Menzoberranzan.

BEWARE DROW PATROLS. THEY'LL SEE YOU BEFORE YOU SEE THEM

Eaten by Mind Flayers

In the world of brain cuisine (sadly, there is one), mind flayers reign as top connoisseurs. To avoid becoming the main course, carry spicy thoughts—they hate that. Apparently, brains full of naughty dreams involving your travel companions give them indigestion. Or vicarious embarrassment. Either way, same result.

Elder brains, rulers of the mind flayers, enjoy long-range eavesdropping and absorbing victims' squishy brains. But Netherstones make them not the brainiest after all. Who needs telepathy when you've got a shiny rock?

Demonic Invasions

You leave one archmage unattended, and next thing you know half the Abyss is popping out of a portal. As the demon lord Demogorgon carves a path of destruction, Underdark residents sigh, thinking they should've stuck to mind flayers. Fortunately, you can play into the fact that demons squabble like most families, except with more rending of flesh.

Have you even visited the Underdark if you haven't been backstabbed?

BEWARE!

The real danger might be your ranger's twitchy index finger. The Underdark's mind tricks make you mistrust yourself, and can transform friends into frenemies—you'll start thinking getting lost isn't so bad compared to dodging "accidental" arrows!

Lost in the Labyrinth

Carved long ago by demon-worshiping dwarves, the Labyrinth allows you to get lost even more badly than regular Underdark getting lost. Here, even angels can't find their way back out.

Haunted by Horrors

Fear the Shadows, literally. These animate shadows sneak up, life-draining touch in tow, innocuous yet terrifying. Ghasts lurk hungrily, adding to the lovely ambiance. And those minotaurs you navigated past? Avoid them again; they might just come back... wearing a new set of bones.

MONSTER SPOTTER'S GUIDE

Undead, but not your regular brainless zombie. Wights are filled with hatred for all living things, and are animated by their desire to commit violence against them. Will drain your life force from your body if given the chance. I've seen it done, and it ain't pretty.

HILL GIANT

WIGHT

As giants go, probably the easiest ones to avoid—they're loud, slow, and extremely single minded. Still, I've encountered ones in the Dalelands who could throw a boulder FAR, so don't get caught out.

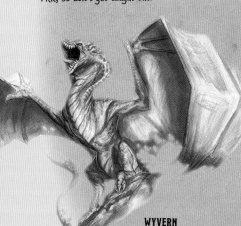

RED WIZARD

WYVERN

It's kind of like a dragon, but not as smart or enchantingly beautiful. We treat them like embarrassing cousins who we don't invite to family gatherings. Watch out for the nasty stinging tail. Gross.

The evil rulers of the land of Thay. Not monsters as such, but certainly monstrous in their lack of basic decency and morals. Their tattoos and clothes show which school of magic they belong to, so look closely (but not TOO closely).

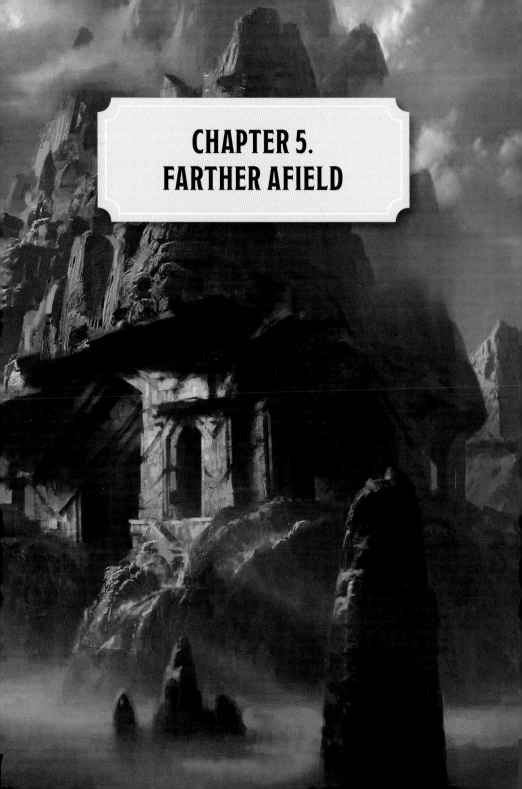

CHAPTER 5.
FARTHER AFIELD

NAUTICAL VENTURES

❋

SETTING SAIL IN FAERÛN: MORE ADVENTURING, LESS DROWNING!

The sea has called many an adventurer to trade, explore, or flee in-laws, and told just as many to stay home, landlubber. From mastering ship signals to deciphering a mermaid's moody flipper wave, the seas are full of quirks. Learn fast, or swim faster!

A sextant: not as much fun as it sounds, but better than a compass.

To reach vibrant, tucked-away ports, find a ship that laughs at tight spaces and rough seas!

Hiring your Sea Ride

If you find haggling tough on land, just wait until you're negotiating with a captain who's half-convinced you bring bad luck or worse—barnacles. Use the dwarf in your party to make the approach, not the red dragonborn (I know from experience that fire-breathing raises costs!). Ensure the wizard's "almost new" ship doesn't teleport to unexpected places. And do pay extra for the anti-siren package!

A stowaway trying not to get caught in the act

Worst case: Sneak aboard at dusk, pack snacks, avoid rats, listen closely, find a quiet barrel, and hold your breath!

BEWARE!

Many and varied dangers await on and below the seas. Sure, that friendly-looking mermaid offered directions, but can she be trusted? Sea hags wait in their caves to feast on your flesh, while dragon turtles have a nasty habit of mistaking ships for dinner. Storm giants? Turns out they're not big on small talk. Pirates? Good times, if you fancy parting with your gold. Plus, that ghost ship could host actual ghosts, its crew seeking to add to their number (don't join them—they don't pay). Those luminous shoals may hide ancient Netherese cities below, drowned and waiting for the unsuspecting. And even the most seasoned traveler can succumb to simple seasickness. Again. I won't say who, but his name starts with "V" and ends with "Why didn't you let me bring the Potion of Lesser Restoration?"

CHARTING A COURSE

1

Know before you go: Acquire a map and familiarize yourself with the timing of the tides. Argue about it endlessly with your companion. Finally, listen to the captain you hired to sail the ship for you.

2

Navigate: Once out at sea, you need a sextant, not a compass. Watch your companion aim the sextant at a star, note the angle, check the sea chart, and realize you're still lost. Such brilliance, so often wasted.

Underwater Politics

The fish-like sahuagin claim all seas, constantly clashing with the sea elves, who profoundly disagree. When even the powerful, peacemaking tritons lose their patience, you know it's serious. If you want to play in these waters, bone up on your sea deities and pack diplomacy skills!

A SAHUAGIN

...means "I'm really annoyed at you." Immediately stop.

Fast-flicking tail.

Show respect by reacting correctly to merfolk gestures.

CALIMSHAN

FAR MORE SIGNIFICANT THAN JUST THE PLACE WHERE ALL YOUR EMERALD RINGS COME FROM

Packed with genie wars and great civilizations, Calimshan's history books are so thrilling they make epic tales jealous. While the North was still doodling in the margins of magic, Calimshan wrote the whole spellbook.

Before Calim and Memnon, two rival ancient genies, were imprisoned—yet again—they turned Calimshan into their sandbox of wars and sorcery. Their elementally-empowered servants, the genasi, then ruled in their absence, until the people of Calimshan finally overthrew them and took control of their own fate.

The Calim Desert, where every grain of sand tells a story, some sing ballads, and others just critique your outfit.

A CALISHITE MONK

Unlike this monk, I'd suggest full skin coverage. The Calim Desert's version of a light breeze comes with a side of sandpaper.

The fire genasi served Memnon, while the air genasi served Calim. And after their rulers mysteriously disappeared, they just served themselves.

Yes, he has a rope to hold up his pants. Better show some respect anyway, just to be safe.

FIRE GENASI

AIR GENASI

Watch out for great rocs! It isn't fun getting dive-bombed by bird droppings the size of a tent.

While the genies still ruled, getting into Almraiven was harder than convincing a dragon to share treasure.

KEY LOCATIONS

Calimport One of the greatest cities in all of Faerûn, where the obscenely wealthy live right on top of the obscenely poor and alliances change as frequently as the desert winds. Navigating the court of the Emperor Syl–Pasha requires more than just a keen sense of direction.

Memnon The great but–not–quite–as–great–as–Calimport city named for a rival genie, where sultans rule, viziers pull the strings, and beggars join guilds for better rates.

Almraiven Where mages outwit genies and the gnolls run the bars. It once stood as Calimshan's last human city against the genasi warlords.

The Marching Mountains A mountain range that runs along the northern border of Calimshan, separating it from the realms to the north such as Thethyr, Amn, and the cities of the Sword Coast.

DO / DO NOT

- **DO** try the local cuisine, but keep in mind that "mild" here means "only slightly magical."
- **DO** smile and nod the hundredth time a resident tells you they have family in Baldur's Gate, even though you live a fortnight's journey from it.
- **DO NOT** call a Memnonian a "Calishite"—that's like mistaking a dragon for a lizard.

After showing the genasi warlords the door, which just happened to be a portal to another plane, humans and tieflings have been steering the Calim caravan, hoping not to crash it again, while the remaining genasi give dubious directions. Rulers, or pashas, orchestrate their domains, where status isn't measured by mere piles of gold, but by the art of lounging atop them.

THE DALELANDS

BIRTHPLACE OF BRAVE RANGERS, WHERE THE ONLY COMMON GROUND IS THE GROUND

A rather loose alliance of towns, the Dales tend to agree to disagree, loudly. Even so, they are united in their suspicion of strangers and what lurks in the Arch Wood. Their greatest exports? Timber, grain, a grumpy attitude, and me.

If you don't mind the hauntings, Arch Wood amazes with its old oaks—old because the owlbears enforce a strict "no-chopping" policy. These accidental rangers with claws and beaks inspired me to become one (a ranger, not an owlbear). Nearby, the River Ashaba gives life to towns like Feather Falls, where travelers come to watch feathers fall, and leave sorely disappointed.

Caravans face ambushes so often it's a toss-up whether the roads need protection from bandits or the other way around!

The Dalelands cozy up to more mighty neighbors, but unfortunately their handy connecting roads and bountiful countryside have often made invasion seem like a fun idea.

KEY INFO

Shadowdale: Where Archmage Elminster might be your next-door neighbor, popping over with his pointed hat for a cup of tea. He's delightful. I should've been his apprentice.

Mistledale: A dale with a giant meteoric scar filled with peaceful farmlands, occasionally interrupted by the odd wayward goblin from Thunder Peaks thinking he's found an easy target.

Scardale: A beautiful seaside locale where the most unexpected thing is the suspiciously cheerful "No Invasion or Plagues This Week!" sign.

Archendale: Most well defended (and arrogant) of the Dales. Home of the Archenrider army, and led by three anonymous warriors known as the Three Swords.

Not just a haven for rangers, the Dales serve as a crossroads for all sorts of folk (how else would a dragonborn end up among humans?). The Harpers, secretive agents of the downtrodden, abound, while the evil Zhentarim are considered mortal enemies of all the Dales. Even the Cormanthyr elves respect their old pacts with the Dalelanders, like not leaving their unicorns in someone else's meadow.

Myth Drannor: capital of the ancient elven nation of Cormanthyr. Is it a ruin? Is it thriving? Visit and find out!

PERILS OF ANAUROCH

To the north of the Dalelands lies Anauroch, a once-lush empire turned into a desert thanks to magical hubris. It's now a sea of dynamic, ever-shifting dunes that want to be close personal friends with you forever and ever and ever. Tips for crossing: stay hydrated, avoid the midday sun like a vampire avoids morals, and try not to trip over any Netherese ruins buried in the sand. There are some things in the Realms that should stay buried.

Better to stub a toe on a buried spire than to pocket Netherese trinkets— nothing like cursed relics to spice up your life!

In Thay, the undead work daily shifts and the liches hold boring staff meetings that are literal torture. Truly the banality of evil.

THAY

WHERE MAGIC REIGNS SUPREME AND THE LIVING ENVY THE PERKS OF BEING A ZOMBIE

East of the Dalelands lies this sinister magocracy, where the Red Wizards are dying (literally) to gain power under an undead lich regent. Thay's commitment to "excellence" could almost be impressive if it didn't include industrial-scale murder and necromancy.

If you're hunting for magical bargains, Thay's merchants, lacking any sort of morality, trade in a variety of sought-after goods, from enchanted amulets that guarantee a good night's sleep to ornate staffs that can conjure minor illusions of being anywhere but Thay. The only catch? The price tag might include your soul.

WHO GOT THIS CLOSE?!

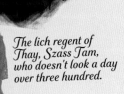

The lich regent of Thay, Szass Tam, who doesn't look a day over three hundred.

DO / DO NOT

- **DO NOT** visit. Really, why are you here? Even Volo draws the line at Thay, and believe me, he does not easily draw lines. Or his own baths.

- **DO NOT** trade with the merchants. It may be a nice enchanted ring, but you have to ask: enchanted by whom?

- **DO** find allies—fast. There aren't any to find, but it's nice to dream.

Commoners in Thay aim high— some literally, as apprentice spellcasters; others figuratively, as in "let's try not to become undead street sweepers."

The Red Wizards sit atop Thay's status pyramid, flaunting their arcane skills like peacocks with spellbooks. Wear red at your peril.

Some Red Wizards left Thay, opposing Szass—proof that even black hearts can change... slightly.

SYMBOL OF THAY

GLADIATORS AND CAPTIVES

GLADIATOR SWORD

Whether captured in battle, locked up for debts, or punished for having hair, the real reason for imprisonment in Thay hinges on cold profit, with each unfortunate soul a mere ledger entry in the Red Wizards' grand, monstrous scheme. The alternative to a dungeon? Trained to perfection, Thay's gladiators, from minotaurs to lizardfolk, serve as the go-to distraction from the ever–present fear of eternal undeath.

Often used as political pawns, some gladiators turn to adventuring for the freedom it offers (and the fewer chances of being incinerated for entertainment.)

MONSTER SPOTTER'S GUIDE

JABBERWOCK

These trickster fey love causing trouble. They're sly, crafty, and they'll prank anyone, anywhere, anytime. I once woke up to find my pack had been replaced with an angry goblin. Classic Boggle.

I've never actually seen one of these—I've only seen drawings, and frankly they're all terrible. It seems a bit dragon-like, but I'm not sure if it's related to my scaly kin. Either way, apparently it will track you relentlessly until it eats you, and will babble at you mercilessly the whole time.

BOGGLE

QUICKLING

Devious and cruel, Quicklings are lightning fast. Most of the time you'll just see a blur. They'll stab at your legs with their daggers, then speed out of reach again. They usually hide in forested areas, so eyes on the trees!

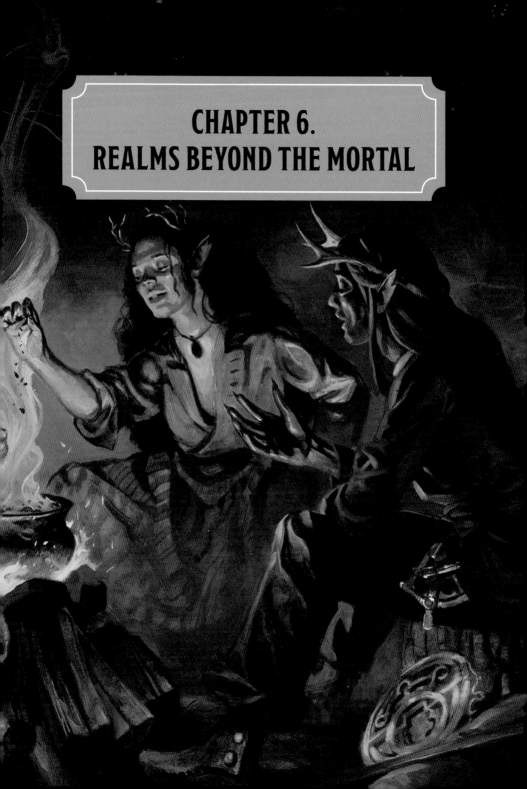

CHAPTER 6.
REALMS BEYOND THE MORTAL

LOCATION

THE FEYWILD

LIKE THAT DREAM WHERE EVERYTHING GLOWS... AND TRIES TO KIDNAP YOU

In this wild, whimsical mirror to the mundanity of the Material Plane, eladrin frolic, pixies scheme, and the unwary might waltz for decades, bewitched by a dryad's smile. Proceed with glee—and caution. Time here is as tricky as a sprite's promise.

The landscape of the Feywild shifts as quickly as court allegiances. Sulk, and the earth might just frown back. Chuckle, and don't be startled when rocks smirk along. Queen Titania rules the Seelie, or Summer, Court with warmth, while the Winter Court chills under their nameless Queen's gaze. You could even find my old friend dear Tasha, —aka the Witch Queen—in her domain of Prismeer, if you need a laugh.

Know your fey: pixies cause pranks, sprites wield tiny spears, dryads blend with trees, and nymphs charm with beauty—each fey distinct, from playful tricksters to stoic guardians.

It might be a small, fluffy, purring kitten, but it's still a displacer beast. Keep your distance.

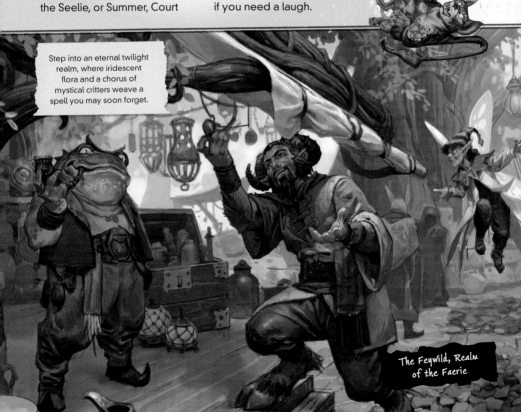

Step into an eternal twilight realm, where iridescent flora and a chorus of mystical critters weave a spell you may soon forget.

The Feywild, Realm of the Faerie

HARENGON: (FUR)BALLS OF ENERGY AND FUN TIMES. I LIKE THEM A LOT.

The Feywild wields the most powerful and creative charms. Here, a bewitched giant spider enlightens fey critters on not being lunch. A story shared, a meal spared.

Summer eladrin, an elf-like fey

MEETING TASHA: DO / DO NOT

Tasha dons the hat, cackles on cue, and puts on grand, witchy theatrics for naive visitors.

• **DO NOT** accept gifts the first three times offered. Accept the fourth time to avoid giving offense.

• **DO NOT** ask for favors. You may not like the price.

• **DO** call her Iggwilv. No, I will not tell you how to pronounce it. She reserves "Tasha" for old friends.

• **DO** laugh at her jokes, or she will make you.

GETTING THERE

Finding the Feywild's door is a game of chance. You might waltz through a mushroom circle or duck under a gnarled tree. Next thing you know, you're in fairyland, with nary a clue how you got there (or how to get back).

For a sure thing, find the traveling Witchlight Carnival, which comes from the Feywild and crosses over to the Realms on rare occasions. Outwit the chiefs or nab the Witchlight Watch for a backstage pass. In the Hall of Illusions, utter the magic words, touch the misty glass, and soon you'll be tumbling into a world of Feywild frolics.

FEYWILD DINING

FROM FRUIT TARTS TO FAIRY CAKES: AN EPICUREAN ADVENTURE (WITH OCCASIONAL PERIL)

Blink dogs herd berries that scamper on tiny legs, and dryads craft them into tarts. Meanwhile, a satyr plays a tune that coaxes the vegetables to chop themselves. Elves bake loaves of bread that rise to the table. Here, the farm-to-table experience isn't just fresh; it's practically sprinting to your plate.

KEY INFO

Flattery will get you everywhere: Compliment a sprite's wings or best a harengon in a limerick duel and you'll enjoy an enchanted evening munching on laughter-marinated leaves.

Bring Your Own Brew: You're expected to bring some of Feywild's finest. Lucky for you, Sprucebark Quaff flows freely in many fey waterways.

Traveler's "taverns": If you find an elusive fey inn, prepare for a banquet illusion that only fills a pixie's appetite for mischief!

At a Feywild farmstead, you're hired if you can knead dough to the satyr's tune and not eat the giant sentient pumpkins. Unfortunately, you're paid in daydreams and blinkblossoms.

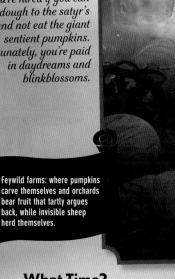

Feywild farms: where pumpkins carve themselves and orchards bear fruit that tartly argues back, while invisible sheep herd themselves.

What Time?

You might sit down for a mid-morning midnight snack, where faerie dragons serve tea that tastes like sunsets. By afternoon's first moonrise, it's time for a reverse supper as the fey present you with an appetizer for tomorrow's breakfast. Time, much like the cuisine, is a playful trickster here.

Only one of these has teeth. Guess which.

Mind your manners: Some plants prefer greetings before becoming your Feywild salad!

Volo insisted I try the "giant snail" in the Feywild. Perhaps the aftermath of a dodgy toadstool snack on his part. Note: Verify sightings with sober second opinions.

BEWARE!

Feywild feasts can be perilous! Darker fey serve up dishes that deceive. One minute you're savoring a starfruit tart, the next you're a toad. Nectar of the Nymphs? Perhaps for the fae. For you, three sips in, you might end up seeing into other, less savory, realms. There's the occasional Casserole of Confusion, and that roast could very well be flavored with redcap blood. How hungry are you, truly?

Fey pastry musts: Fairy cakes, pixie pies, and sprite scones. Tip: Avoid ones that giggle when bitten. They bite back!

I nibbled a pixie pie; the chuckling cherries nipped me back! Hope I'm as tasty as they were.

They say the fruit picks itself, preferring the company of your plate to the bush.

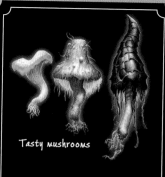

Tasty mushrooms

A HERO'S FEAST

1

Appetizer: Start with a bioluminescent lichen licked by will-o'-the-wisp flames, served on a leaf of silver that's been argued over by two pixies convinced it's a mirror.

2

Entree: Dine by the light of your meal with glow-in-the-dark mushroom risotto. It's been whispered to radiance by an eladrin with a penchant for culinary drama, ensuring no diner loses their spoon in the dark.

3

Final course: A pudding so stubbornly bioluminescent it's escorted by grumbling boggarts wearing sun goggles, nestled in a pastry shell crafted under a full moon with just a hint of giggling sprite magic.

Homicidal redcaps

THE SHADOWFELL

LIKE THE MATERIAL PLANE, BUT SHADOWY AND WITH MORE FROWNS

In this dark mirror of the Realms, the sun's too shy to shine bright and trees mope because they miss their colorful leaves. Nature itself took a solemn vow of gloom, with every breeze sighing in despair, and streams murmuring in sorrow. Even the rocks seem to be lost in thought.

The Shadowfell's societies throw the most hair-raising gatherings, where ghost stories are small talk, and they swap tales about how they survived the previous night. Traditions include not smiling (it's considered showing off) and customs include animating the dead.

Whether it's a prison, a ghost metropolis, or your unconscious mind, it still probably looks like a crumbling castle.

Gloomwrought: the melancholy metropolis where Prince Rolan rules and merchant nobles vie to see who cares the least.

To reach the Shadowfell, find a shadow crossing, step into the gloom, and tada! You're in a monochrome echo of the Material Plane. Traverse twisted landscapes and explore Evernight, the Shadowfell's necromancer-laden answer to Neverwinter.

The Fortress of Memories: the Raven Queens icy domain, where souls bundle up before the afterlife's next adventure.

Shadowfell spirit

Shadow dragon

Shadow mastiff

Nightwalker

All who call the Shadowfell home are slowly twisted by its dark energies. Nightmarish creatures, like spirits and nightwalkers, excel in the art of surprise cameos during your late-night ale runs. Once true dragons, shadow dragons rule their domains in silence, like they did in the Material Plane before getting stuck here. But quit giving your dragonborn companion suspicious side-eyes; none of us have morphed into a shadow dragonborn... yet.

DO/DO NOT

- **DO** pack light, the gloom adds weight.

- **DO NOT** rely on maps or compasses. Landmarks often hide to avoid visitors.

- **DO** visit your own home's shadow twin. Sure, whatever lives there could kill you, but who doesn't love seeing their childhood dolly glaring with malevolent eyes?

- **DO NOT** linger, or you may stop caring about your comrades, or worse, treasure.

How shadar-kai look when tallying your heartaches for their queen.

RAVENLOFT

In a dark corner of the Shadowfell stands Ravenloft and its "Domains of Dread," each a villain's pocket-sized, personalized nightmare, tailor-made by the Dark Powers to confine them. Regrettably, they also house innocent bystanders trying to enjoy their supper with slightly less dread.

Shadar-kai, the Raven Queen's teleporting envoys: elves with less emotion and a touch of the grave.

Daylight in Ravenloft is merely night wearing a flimsy disguise, and frankly, it's not fooling anyone.

Barovia's grand entrance sets the mood for all of Ravenloft's domains. Famed? Perhaps. Impressive? Undeniably. Welcoming? Never.

RAVENLOFT
✠

THE REALM THAT MAKES HAUNTED HOUSES LOOK LIKE CHILD'S PLAY

Welcome to Ravenloft, where castle views and misty landscapes are as common as the ever-present sense of looming catastrophe. Prepare to sharpen your stakes, run for your life, and try to survive until what passes for dawn. It's the perfect place to brood, or, perhaps, regret your travel choices!

Strahd leaves his storied castle for a nightly "terrorize the town" joyride!

Lean in, to learn the secret of Ravenloft's Darklords. Dark Powers turned these scoundrels into star prisoners, each trapped in their own personalized gothic domain. With countless innocents also dragged in (if you are reading this desperately, you among them), it's a dreadful affair!

Some Darklords shun thrones, but not the vampire Count Strahd von Zarovich of Barovia. He embraces the cliché with unparalleled brooding gusto!

Blood of the Vine

Near Strahd's Castle in Barovia, rebels whisper and spies snoop, while the barkeep just hopes someone remembers to pay their tab.

The Silvered Mirror

In the domain known as Darkon, mirrors adorning a mansion–turned–inn reflect impending doom as the deadly fog known as the Shroud consumes everything. Never mind, don't stay there.

Bouncing Bard Inn

The bartender pours, the bard croons, and the cat caterwauls. All night. No sleep in Kartakass, domain of bards, until the sweet embrace of fame!

Mordenheim's Villa

With shifting walls and automaton furniture, this lodging offers a "be–eaten–by–your–own–bedroom" experience in Lamordia.

DO / DO NOT

- DO enjoy the scenic fog, but watch out, for it might enjoy you right back.

- DO try the Blood of the Vine Tavern's house wine; it's almost worth the incessant vampire spawn surveillance. Almost.

- DO NOT extend or accept dinner invites; residents may misinterpret "having you for dinner."

Braving the Mists

The Mists, Ravenloft's notorious border guards, appear at domains' edges and envelop the lands. The Darklords wield power over them, transporting wayfarers and cloaking dangers. To find a Mist talisman, try sifting through old, dramatic relics, like a vampire's diary or a lich's love letters. With this odd compass in hand, you just might outmaneuver the Mists' masters. "Happy" fog-wading, adventurer!

107

DEALING WITH VAMPIRES AND OTHER NIGHTMARES

A GUIDE TO OUTWITTING FANGS AND SIDESTEPPING THE SPECTRAL

While vampires pose a constant threat in Ravenloft, the realm's woes don't end there. Nature's turned traitor, hags peddle perilous pies, and mist horrors add an eerie touch. Moreover, corrupt nobles play deadly games of power, and deception is the local pastime. Straightforward bloodsucking can almost seem refreshingly honest!

KEY INFO

Soul Searchers: Ghosts love to possess living souls, and they're not picky. Any warm body will do for these incorporeal freeloaders.

By all means be a chum and release them by taking care of unfinished business. But first make sure you're not the business they want to finish.

Ask spirits clear yes or no questions. "You didn't steal the port wine, right?" leaves everyone confused.

"yes, I didn't"

A spirit board guides your hands to unveil the unseen. Take care, though, for not all spirits play nice.

Or "no, I did"

ZOMBIES, WHEN BAFFLED

Meet Barovian hag Morgantha: baker of dubious desserts that turn sweet dreams into terrifying, pastry-wrapped nightly adventures!

Undead Encounters

Equip yourself with holy water, a trusty enchanted blade, and a relentless cleric, and you'll handle undead assailants as confidently as a bard chasing an endless keg of mead!

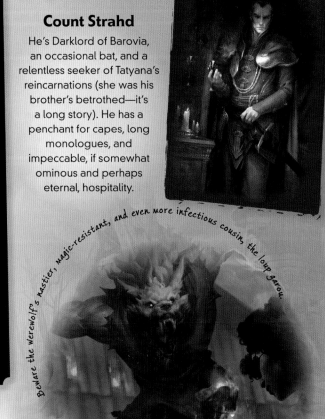

Strahd's nightmare steed, *Bucephalus*, showcases its silent gallops and dramatic, yet somehow also silent, neighs.

VAMPIRE SURVIVAL TIPS

If a charming neighbor knocks on your door, asking to borrow a cup of blood—er, sugar—resist the urge to invite them in for a nightcap. Vampires aren't being polite; they actually need an invitation to enter.

Vampires and running water go together like trolls and logic puzzles. If you've got a moat, fill it up. If you don't have a moat, really, why don't you? Moats are great.

Vampires can both turn into bats and summon battalions of bats. If you want to play Guess the Vampire, try wearing a collarless shirt. If one bat seems particularly interested in you, congratulations, you've found your vampire!

Count Strahd

He's Darklord of Barovia, an occasional bat, and a relentless seeker of Tatyana's reincarnations (she was his brother's betrothed—it's a long story). He has a penchant for capes, long monologues, and impeccable, if somewhat ominous and perhaps eternal, hospitality.

Beware the werewolf's nastier, magic-resistant, and even more infectious cousin, the loup garou.

Werewolves

Shapeshifters of legend, werewolves enjoy moonlit strolls, heartfelt howls, and a diet that's definitely not vegetarian. While all are a tad sensitive to silver, not all are evil. A good *remove curse* spell does wonders.

Kartakass, the domain of bards, is particularly plagued by wolves. Outsiders don't realize their lupine aggressors are more than they seem...

MONSTER SPOTTER'S GUIDE

SOLAR
DRAGON

Among the noblest of all dragons, they soar through Wildspace, basking in their freedom to play and explore, and radiating joy and benevolence to all they encounter. Honestly, I'm a little jealous.

These giant insects care only for exploring and hunting. Not good or evil, they just view everything through the lens of predator and prey. And trust me, they'll view you as the latter.

THRI-KREEN

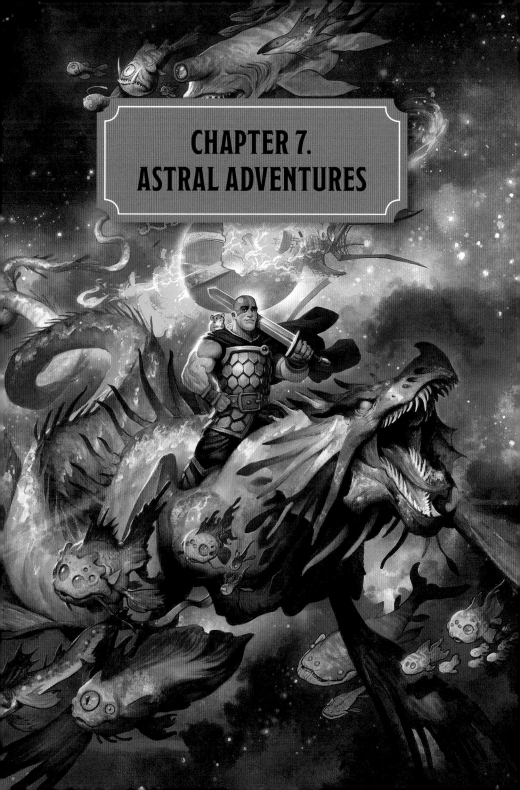

CHAPTER 7.
ASTRAL ADVENTURES

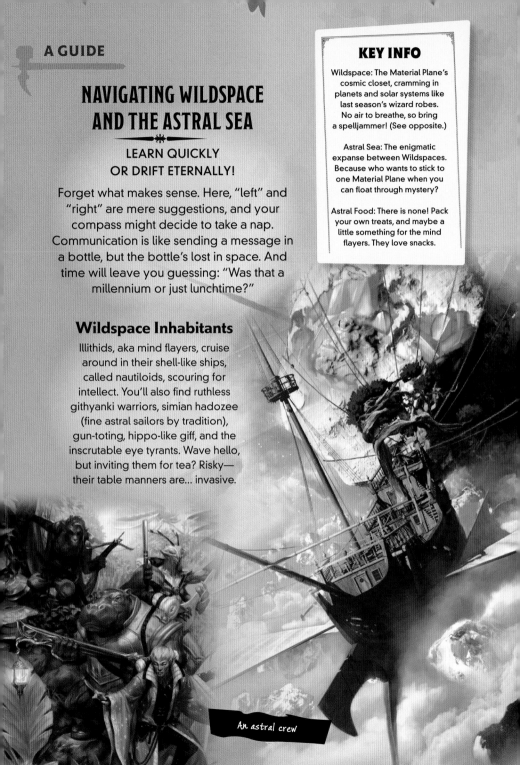

NAVIGATING WILDSPACE AND THE ASTRAL SEA

LEARN QUICKLY OR DRIFT ETERNALLY!

Forget what makes sense. Here, "left" and "right" are mere suggestions, and your compass might decide to take a nap. Communication is like sending a message in a bottle, but the bottle's lost in space. And time will leave you guessing: "Was that a millennium or just lunchtime?"

Wildspace Inhabitants

Illithids, aka mind flayers, cruise around in their shell-like ships, called nautiloids, scouring for intellect. You'll also find ruthless githyanki warriors, simian hadozee (fine astral sailors by tradition), gun-toting, hippo-like giff, and the inscrutable eye tyrants. Wave hello, but inviting them for tea? Risky— their table manners are... invasive.

KEY INFO

Wildspace: The Material Plane's cosmic closet, cramming in planets and solar systems like last season's wizard robes. No air to breathe, so bring a spelljammer! (See opposite.)

Astral Sea: The enigmatic expanse between Wildspaces. Because who wants to stick to one Material Plane when you can float through mystery?

Astral Food: There is none! Pack your own treats, and maybe a little something for the mind flayers. They love snacks.

An astral crew

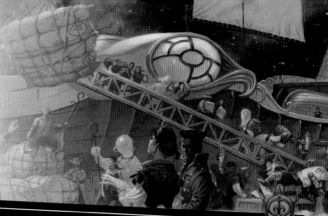

Spelljammers

The spacefaring vessels known as spelljammers are ancient cosmic carpentry at its finest. Obtaining one? Part epic quest, part cosmic haggling. While you're star-hopping, anchoring one may require a whole different spellbook!

SPELLJAMMING BASICS

Spelljamming helms allow spelljammers to be piloted by mere thought. Mount a helm, think "up," and suddenly you're space-bound. Just make sure your thoughts don't drift to that embarrassing moment with your crush in the town square, because guess where you'll end up?

BEWARE!

The only thing worse than fighting pirates is winning and then getting stuck within their foul air envelope. Besides pirates, you'll want to avoid floating debris, sleeping gods, and portals to your mother's house.

A spell for every occasion

No air? In Wildspace you can conjure globes of it, because who wouldn't want a personal, invisible fishbowl? Extra heads? No problem, just make extra bubbles! Perfect for multi-headed parties.

BOO!

This telepathic space hamster is one of Wildspace's greatest adventurers. Unlike his giant space hamster kin, Boo is conveniently travel-sized, and has often protected his sidekick, Minsc, whose instruction of "Go for the Eyes!" proves a surprisingly effective strategy.

A cosmic sandwich with a mixed society upper crust, a gravity plane filling, and an off-limits imprisoned pickle underneath!

THE ROCK OF BRAL

SPELLJAMMING, WILDSPACE, COSMIC MISFITS, AND THE ASTEROID WHERE THEY ALL CONVERGE

What is Wildspace, but a sea of stars, minus water? And what is spelljamming, but sailing through space without wind? Get all the wrong answers on the Rock of Bral, where astral sailors swap tales and misplace moons.

This cosmic bazaar of the bizarre beckons adventurers and entrepreneurs alike. Bral's charm lies in its ability to surprise—one minute you're dodging spells, the next you're critiquing street theater performed by rogue imps. Skip the Rock's underside, not because it's forbidden (though it is), but more because it features crop-tending convicts, not beach resorts!

The asteroids known as the Tears of Selûne, as seen from Faerûn. The Rock of Bral is up there... somewhere.

In the city, laws bend like a contortionist. Every tavernkeeper doubles as a bouncer, and even the local minstrels have perfected the art of the side-eye. Especially by the docks, keep your friends close and your suspicions closer.

DO / DO NOT

- **DO** play nice with Prince Andru: He's so skilled in diplomacy, he could convince a mind flayer to turn vegetarian.

- **DO** hop aboard a spelljammer. You might not get off otherwise.

- **DO NOT** expect a magistrate's intervention. If you were robbed, they'll wonder why you weren't watching hard enough.

- **DO NOT** climb the edges to reach the underside. You might fall... into Wildspace, then keep falling. Use the sewers like a normal person.

Amid this pirate haven a lone temple to Tyr, god of justice stands, home to a band of justice-loving, crime-fighting, unpopular priests, who wage a relentless, oddly unappreciated crusade against the very rogues who call the lawless Rock home.

Tyr: Not good at reading the room.

That is one happy beholder!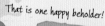

THE HAPPY BEHOLDER TAVERN

A personal favorite of mine. Nestled in the heart of Bral's Low City, this little tavern sees more floating beverages than a wizard's banquet. Here, the only thing stronger than the drinks is the eponymous barkeep Large Luigi's telekinetic gaze!

ELYSIUM A must! The Beastlands, a ranger's paradise, give even the most incompetent hunter a boost, with only a slight chance of turning into a stag by sunset.

THE OUTER PLANES

REALMS WHERE DEITIES MINGLE AND THE LAWS OF PHYSICS POLITELY STEP ASIDE

If the Elemental Planes are the multiverse's raw materials, the Outer Planes are its architects' dreams. Deities sculpt realms with thought and purpose as easily as bards spin tales. Landscapes shift like their ever-changing minds, and distances laugh at logic.

These planes, reflecting good and evil, order and chaos, and every combination thereof, challenge every adventurer to blend in with the plane's vibe or risk feeling like a barbarian at a library—out of place and overly loud. For good times, head to the Upper Planes, though they can be uptight. Still, better by far than the Lower Planes, where the evil inhabitants don't even use coasters.

THE NINE HELLS Avernus boasts lakes of fire, raining ash, and an infernal war that just won't end. It might appear like a family reunion, but with more infernal chains.

MT. CELESTIA On Mount Celestia, the higher you go the better you feel, as angels throw blessings like confetti at a parade.

LIMBO In Limbo, your thoughts fuel the world. Imagine wisely, or that rock might turn into your fiery doom. Here, daydreams have consequences.

MECHANUS In Mechanus, order rules the roost and even thoughts tick in perfect harmony. Spend enough time around the modrons who call this plane home, and even the wildest adventurer might start craving a schedule in this clockwork universe.

WHERE ~~NOT~~ TO STAY

THE ABYSS This is Chaos's answer to the finely ordered evil of the Nine Hells. It's an infinitely layered, constantly shifting hellscape, populated by demons who are less into small talk and more into screaming a battle charge. My recommendation, should you find yourself here, is leave. Leave immediately. And if you're trapped here, well, goodbye!

Each layer of the Abyss is ruled by a demon lord. The Demonweb Pits (layer 66) is the domain of Lolth, the spider queen, who weaves her webs of deceit and danger, turning a simple stroll into a date with eight-legged doom.

LOLTH (IN CASE THERE WAS ANY DOUBT)

There aren't really any survival tips when it comes to demon lords. If you meet one, pray to your god(s) for a quick and painless exit.

117

DEMONS AND OTHER PLANAR BEINGS

DANCE WITH THE DEVIL(S) ENTIRELY AT YOUR OWN RISK

A GLABREZU DIDN'T ACTUALLY POSE FOR THIS

NEITHER DID THIS BALOR DEMON!

Dealing with planar beings? Smile, nod, and never sign anything! Bring a gift, maybe a nice cosmic trinket. If all else fails, run fast, teleport faster, and leave a decoy. Best practice: your soul is not up for barter, so keep it close. Try your pocket!

Marilith (a demon)

Glabrezu (a devil)

These multitaskers of the Abyss juggle swords and schemes with equal flair and ferocity, then kill you.

Deals charm, claws enforce the terms.

Don't pull their tails!

Fiends

In the Lower Planes, the term "fiend" covers many different flavors of evil. Demons thrive amid the chaos of the Abyss, while devils, calling The Nine Hells home, stick to the letter of every infernal contract. The two have been battling each other for a very, *very* long time. Meanwhile, the largely indifferent yugoloths haunt Gehenna and Hades, being bad simply because it's in their job description.

Glabrezu offer deals too good to be true with one appendage and unleash unhappiness with the other five.

Pit fiend (a devil)

Demonic generals, balors are sore losers, dying in a fiery burst rivaling the worst temper tantrum and scorching everything nearby.

Wants to be your pit friend!

"GOOD" DOESN'T MEAN NICE!

Celestials

Hailing from the Upper Planes, celestials are beings who are inherently good. Archons are the stoic cosmic guards, while angels are the more personable winged messengers. Don't be surprised if the archons expect a little reverence and won't laugh at your jokes. Even the angels might only chuckle out of politeness. They've been hearing them for millennia, after all.

An angel planetar

Planetars' shield

Planetars' sword

Modrons

Cogs in the great cosmic clockwork that is the Plane of Mechanus, modrons follow their ruler Primus's orders with the precision of, well, a clock. They chat only with direct colleagues, making it difficult for the latest gossip to really spread. Every 289 years a great modron caravan hits the cosmic road, but precisely what they're up to (or after) no one knows.

BEWARE!

Devils' bargains get a bad reputation because they are, objectively, terrible, but your soul will fare little better if you fail to hold up your end of a bargain with an archon. It may be a bit shinier, though. Think you're safe once you flee the plane? These mighty beings can cross planes with a thought; they will not balk at interrupting you in the privy.

Slaadi

Denizens of Limbo, slaadi are the ultimate chaos enthusiasts, with the strongest toad ruling the pond. Color coordination could save your life: red slaadi will inject you with their spawn, blue will transform you into a slaad yourself, and green will take on your form if you get infected. What's not to love?

And they hatch right out of your companions!

119

SIGIL: CITY OF DOORS

INFINITE DOORS, INFINITE POSSIBILITIES, INFINITE CHANCES TO GET LOST

To visit the planes, do try the floating ring-shaped city of Sigil, where "up" and "down" are merely friendly suggestions. In this bustling hub, traders hawk wares from realms so obscure even the maps gave up. Need a quick trip to the Plane of Water? There's a door for that! But maybe grab a Ring of Water Breathing first.

Stroll Sigil's streets and markets, dodging pitches from centaurs selling everything from dragon-scale gloves to slightly cursed cutlery.

KEY INFO

Local directions: Asking for directions here could lead you on an unexpected two-day adventure... to the same spot.

Surprise weather: It's the only place where you might need a potion of *fire resistance* and snow boots at the same time.

Culinary roulette: Eating out? Brace yourself for dishes that challenge not only taste buds, but also the laws of nature.

Exploration

Go ahead, hop between planes like it's a hobby, but also keep an eye out. If a dabus, one of the Lady's silent cleaning crew, starts "talking" to you in cryptic rebuses, hustle to the closest door—even if it leads to the Plane of Awkward Conversations.

NOT A TALKER ←

The Lady of Pain

The Lady of Pain runs Sigil. She's a mystery wrapped in an enigma, cloaked in spikes. Legends of Her Dread Majesty's power and impartiality abound, but step carefully. Her shadow's the last thing many see before an impromptu banishment to the Maze, Sigil's least fun attraction.

When beings on the Astral Plane feel like eating, they come to Sigil. Fancy a meal from the Nine Hells today? Sigil's diverse doorways mean diverse diners! And diverse eaters—watch you don't end up a meal.

Portal Panics

Portals require peculiar keys—a feather, a song, or your best impression of an owlbear. Some portals demand a command word, often forgotten and replaced with wild guessing. Guess correctly for a jaunt to Elysium; flub it and you're in the Abyss, dodging demon invitations to brunch.

Gravity in Sigil is on a very loose leash.

Track down this portal compass, for a personal "portal-sniffing" blink dog, minus the drool and the barking. Thank me by buying another book.

POINTS IN DIRECTION OF LAST PORTAL YOU WENT THROUGH →

CONCLUSION

WHERE WE BID FAREWELL TO THE REALMS, DODGE THE LAST OWLBEAR, AND WISH YOU MANY MORE HAPPY AND SAFE-ISH ADVENTURES!

—✳—

Really? You made it to the end? I'm surprised you listened to me—and survived in one piece. You ran from your shadow in the Underdark? You took no more than two naps in Elysium? You impress me, maybe not with your wisdom but definitely with your courage.

I admit I enjoyed writing this book for you. It reminded me of all the foolish places I allowed Volo to drag me. I do deeply regret all the potions I drank in order to write it, as I'm starting to feel a bit queasy. From now on, I leave the wordsmithing to Volo. I'll stick to the bow and making sure he doesn't enrage the owlbears (he does it to annoy me, I know it!).

And truly, if you learn nothing else from this book, never travel the realms with Volo. I've had enough. I'm a ranger! I should go find a forest to patrol. And yet instead, here I am.

Consider:

* The late night dinner runs—Volo has another Yawning Portal in his stomach.

* He constantly borrows coin—He dines with lords! Why is he always short one gold piece?

* He snores! He's literally snoring right now.

* He never. Stops. Talking. I no longer question if what he says is true; I only wonder if he will ever stop saying it.

* He can go nowhere without giving quests to adventurers—all to "promote his Guides." But oh, to see the light in his eyes as he hears their tales when they return...

And... he has given me the world. So I sadly, sadly cannot think of any other place I'd rather be than by his side. If you catch me with Volo at the Yawning Portal Inn, please tell me to leave. I won't listen, but at least I'll know you read my book.

If you like my look, take this book to Brian the Swordmaster's Smithy in South Ward, Waterdeep, for a discount!

123

INDEX